DEVIL IN THE CHAIN

A
SUPPLY CHAIN
NOVEL

BY
JAMES
AMOAH

PASCAL EDITIONS

DEVIL IN THE CHAIN

A Supply Chain Business Novel

DEDICATION

To my mother
for her ongoing love and support

And to my father
who could not see this book completed

ACKNOWLEDGEMENTS

Turning my ideas and passion for supply chain into a story has taken longer and been more challenging than I originally thought, but has been more rewarding than I could ever have imagined.

None of this would have been possible without my awesome wife, Sarah. From reading early drafts to giving me advice on the cover to keeping everything else running whilst I indulged my literary ambitions, she was as important to this book getting done as I was. Thank you so so much, dearest.

For being the best and earliest listeners of all my stories and a source of greatest laughter, fun, love and encouragement, I'd like to thank my children, Naomi, Johanna, Benjamin and Jacob—whose names inspired me to write.

For my best of brothers, Joseph and Jones and their wonderful families, who have been and continue to provide unconditionally support and encouragement in all of my pursuits.

To Nick Everitt and Mike Teasdale for taking the time to invest and guide my early supply chain career development, when the profession had not yet gained that name.

To my inspirational Johnson and Johnson UK Board

and colleagues - Vince Pender, Will Fin, Clare Lee, Chris Belton, Clare Sicklen, Vittorio Rosetti, Carl Dempsey, Neil Dickinson, Darren Fowler, Vanessa Dawkins, Samantha Horton, Caroline Stevens and Steve Searle—as we dared to "Go for Process Excellence Gold" and achieve it. This shaped forever my goal to build and be a part of great teams.

To Filip De Keersmaecker, from whom I learnt the discipline and deliberate practice needed to be truly competent in Supply Chain.

To Neil Ryding for teaching me to not only set Big Hairy Audacious Goals (BHAG) but how to mobilise the entire organization to over-deliver on them.

To J.V. Wulf, Kieran Gallahue, Manoj Parmar, Jean-Michel Deckers, Hans Melotte, Andrew Thompson, Mark Branson, Daniel Buzaglo, Juan Jose Gonzalez, for your friendship, business and commercial advice, and for reaffirming my belief that great leaders can exhibit humility.

To Daniel Pettifer from whom I learnt courage and how leadership motivation can achieve above and beyond expectations.

To Mario Reis , Bibi Knoetze, Sue Nocks, Charles Etienne, Jerome Auvinet, Dominic Siddal, Boris Eckstein, Tiago Caldeira, Raffaele DeCecco, Nicolas Gery, Olivier Sosso, Evelyn Church, Glynnis Prain, Pascal Jenny, Vianney Dale,Bhavin Shah, Maria Jose-Justicia Lopez, Ashish Jawadiwar, Ignacio (Nacho) Cuevas, Delphine Surget, Solene Croguennoc-Carre, Eric Dumont, Angela Dauta Brito, Siebe Talma, Jean Leroux, Rishi Rishi, Thiago

Assumpcao and the amazing team at Coty and on the Exit TSA and 1-1-1 Program, who led and delivered a business transformation in the beauty industry that was remarkable and will need a whole book on its own. Your passion and energy were truly inspirational.

To Helmut Leitner, who since our first implementation of S&OP in J&J, 15 years ago—yes, that long—has supported me in the more recent establishment of the Council of Supply Chain Management Professionals (CSCMP) Round Table Switzerland, and who has been a constant, reliable and trusted friend exhibiting high integrity. I thank all the CSCMP RT Switzerland Board for their continued passion and ambition to make the network a success.

To Martin Christopher, Emeritus Professor of Marketing and Logistics, for his many insights and observations on current and future supply chain challenges.

To Michael Hugos and Steve Koji for reigniting my Simulation modeling passion and making it so much more enjoyable than when I had to learn it for Operational Research (OR). To Ibrahim Isshak (Jalal), a friend who has provided continued reminders of Ghana life today with insights on its cocoa farming methods.

To Joelle Mayrargue, Benjamin Lefang, Isabelle Rossigneux, Hugh Anderson. Thank you for our many long Lancaster days, working, being creative, and planning what we would do when we all grow up.

To Professor Dr. Engineering, Katharina Luban, for challenging my thinking by helping me question assumptions.

To all the individuals that I cannot list here but that I have had the opportunity to lead, be led by, or watch their leadership from afar, I want to say thank you for being the inspiration for this book.

DEVIL
IN
THE
CHAIN

Chapter One

Everything Or Nothing

1

Johanna entered the boardroom of Chococoa Enterprises Limited.

It was as she remembered. The long oval table, like a sea of polished British oak; the elegant smell of the plush black leather chairs; the avant-garde Swedish design of the inset lighting, the subtly discreet controls.

Only there were no frowning Executive Directors, no enthusiastic consultants, no PowerPoints unfolding across the darkened screen in the background. The person she would have liked to see there more than anyone else was not there either. Her father.

Only the rest of the family.

And *Nicola*.

Nicola, and Chris from finance. *Nicola*, in the President's chair.

Johanna tried to keep her lip from curling. As a child she had thought of that chair as a throne—her father's throne. After his stroke, her mother, Naomi, became the legal owner of the company and had taken the chair. At first. She would hold court from it, regally, listening to input from family members and from close business associates and advisors, and upon reflection announce her rulings and commissions.

Now Naomi sat to the left, Chris to the right.

Nicola had taken the central spot.

Naomi looked at her daughter Johanna and smiled.

"You're late," noted Nicola. "As usual."

"I stopped at the hospital," said Johanna to Naomi. "To see Father."

"Let's get started," said Nicola.

Nicola handed out several folders.

The first went to Naomi. The next folder went to her brother Benjamin. Benjamin Anan, was a young barrister in London. Still in his twenties, he was already handling several prominent clients as well as the company business. He too smiled at Johanna. A broad smile— he was genuinely happy to see her. He was a bright, positive sort of person and he found people continually entertaining. Superbly dressed as always, a benevolence and amusement always seemed to play across his intelligent, insightful eyes. He clearly anticipated some fun. Johanna was a trouble-maker—his favorite kind of entertainment.

Across from him sat her brother Jacob. Jacob tossed her a smile and a wave. Jacob was eighteen and handsome, and had the ambitious innocent look of a young man dreaming of great things and not yet scarred or strengthened by the experience and struggles of going after them. His school performance so far had been stellar, and he was on the point of entering any one of a dozen prestigious universities—or jumping on a motorbike and backpacking through Europe for a lark. He could go in any direction, and had not yet decided on which.

She loved them both. And they her. And neither of them generally showed up to such meetings, from which she herself was normally politely banned.

Why were they here? What was all this about?

"These documents are not to be discussed with anyone, nor are they to leave this room," said Nicola. "They've been prepared by Christopher and myself for the immediate members of the family only. Please review the details and hand them back to me after you've concluded."

"What's in them?" said Benjamin

"We've received a sealed offer to buy the business. It's my recommendation as chief officer that we take it."

"*What?*" cried Johanna.

"We're selling the company?" said Benjamin.

"If you'll examine the enclosed spreadsheets—"

"*Damn* the spreadsheets," said Johanna. "You want to sell the business? Father spent his entire *life* building this business. Building it for *us*. For us and *our* children."

A flicker of disdain passed across Nicola's otherwise strikingly beautiful features, the *look* that had put her and their firm Chococoa on the covers of financial magazines and into popular talk shows and interviews; the cool aristocratic look that helped Nicola unlock the door to corporate celebrity. It had no effect on Johanna. Nicola always reminded Johanna a bit of the Vulcans in *Star Trek*, repressing themselves as they aspired to pure logic. She had been with Chococoa almost from the time that Johanna's father had come to Great Britain from Ghana. Even so, no one seemed to really know what went on underneath that icy facade.

But to Johanna, there was no mystery: Nicola was only a sterile surface, playing the game of business as a series of coldly calculated moves laid out with crushing certainty on endless Excel documents, bar graphs and pie charts.

"*If* I may continue—?"

"*Mother!*" said Johanna, turning to Naomi.

Naomi sighed. Legally, on paper, Naomi made the final decisions on everything. But she was not a businessperson: her life was in the academic community. After Michael had had his paralyzing stroke, she added the task of caregiver to her list, and cared for Michael at their home. But she knew that she had neither the time nor skills to run a business operation hands-on. In practice, she delegated day-to-day operations and authority to those who seemed best suited to execute company policies, for the most part people set in place by her incapacitated husband Michael.

And so she had delegated the leadership spot to Nicola, Michael's favorite and his former Director of Marketing. It had seemed a wise decision. The firm's growth under Nicola had been—till recently—meteoric. Nonetheless, from the very beginning, Johanna had chafed against her leadership and criticized Nicola every step of the way. And in response, Nicola delegated less and less authority to Johanna, finally allotting her no authority whatsoever. Their views on business operations could not be more opposed, and every board meeting became a pitched battle of argument and counter-argument.

And so, after a blistering exchange across the very same table over two years ago, Johanna had stalked out, resigned her nominal position, and became Supply Chain Manager at another company.

"Please, Johanna, dear," said Naomi. "Hear Nicola out."

Johanna opened her mouth to protest again. But closed it. She sat back in her seat, her arms crossed.

"Thank you—Naomi," said Nicola.

Nicola looked around, lifted a clicker, clicked it. The screen behind her erupted into her customary halo of charts and graphs.

"It's very simple," she began. "Profitability has been declining for the past two years. Significantly. Costs are rising. Expenditures are high. The continuing ripple effects from Brexit are unpredictable, but projections are deeply negative. Our main immediate problem is that the futures market is in free fall. The financial fallout from that has been devastating. Not only to ourselves: our Partners and suppliers are being impacted as well, and are proving… difficult. The documents will explain all this in detail. We've had to take on deeper bank loans to cover continuing cash flow issues. And we've survived. But change to higher interest rates has put us into negative cash flow. If things continue as they are, the firm will be facing certain bankruptcy within three to six months."

She looked everyone at the table in the eye to communicate the seriousness of the situation.

"There have always been major companies interested in purchasing our operation. One such potential buyer, which declines to identity itself, has issued a remarkably handsome offer that will leave everyone here *very* well off indeed. Chris?"

Chris cleared his throat. Despite a somewhat fumbling manner and a face like the young Bill Gates, Chris was Chief Financial Officer. He had risen from being the company resident computer nerd, to crunching the financial data exclusively, to handling all financial operations, which had become overwhelmingly computerized. Where the human touch was needed, Benjamin would be called in to speak with bankers and investors. Chris' social ineptitude was massive. Nicola's dramatic sweep dissipated as he started hemming and hawing about company investments, fluctuating loan rates, derivative investments, credit swaps.

"Chris, I wonder if you could keep this as non-technical as possible?" said Naomi. "I want Jacob in particular to see the full picture clearly."

Chris blinked. He was good at his job, but radiated the autism of the techie. He sometimes had issues translating financials—or even a casual "hello"—into simple English. Surprisingly he was often able to put it into somewhat over-simplified English.

"Jacob," said Chris, "a business starting out is like a person starting out. They don't have enough money to buy a house, so they get a job and rent an apartment. The money from the job pays for the apartment till they save enough to buy a home of their own. But they can't afford to lose that job. If the stream of income stops, they can't pay the rent. And out they go."

Jacob smiled and nodded. "I *did* pass my school GCSE's, you know, Chris."

Chris, humorless, blinked at Jacob through almost comically thick eyeglass lenses, and continued.

"Right. Well, when a business starts out, it doesn't always have money to buy offices and factories and equipment and pay employees. So it goes to a bank. The bank gives them the money they need, if it believes the company will generate enough profit over time to pay them back and pay them back regularly with interest. This company did that. But there was a drop in the revenue flow after your father had his stroke. Nicola managed to reverse that, significantly—"

Johanna snorted.

"But the negative trend has returned. And it's deepened. We've had to go to the bank and take out more loans to compensate. If we liquidate now—if we sell the company on the terms offered by the buyer—

we can pay all the company debts and there will still millions of pounds left to divide among the family. Many millions of pounds. If we *don't* take the offer, we'll have to take out even further loans in the next few months to stay afloat. And if the business continues to decline after that, paying off our debts to the bank may be impossible. It could leave the family with nothing. With less than nothing— in deep lifelong dept. It might even impact your father's medical therapies."

Johanna slapped both hands on the table.

"I *told* you this would happen," said Johanna

Nicola ignored her. "So. Let us consider our options—"

"I warned *all* of you."

"—after Johanna throws her usual infantile fit."

"You've never understood what it is to run a business," said Johanna.

"And yet I *have* run a business," said Nicola, "this business, for the past few years now, and on the whole quite successfully."

" 'On the whole.' Until now!"

"External factors—"

" 'External factors'! You people in *marketing*—in *finance*," she said, throwing an angry glance at Chris. "You think a business is all about crunching numbers."

Nicola nodded. She had heard all this before. Let Johanna have her little tantrum, give her little speech. Then business could proceed.

"And what *is* it all about, Johanna, if not profit?" said Nicola, glancing pointedly at her simple but elegant wristwatch.

"A business is about *things*. About *growing* things. *Making* things. *Moving* things. Giving people the things they *need*. To you, it's not about the product at all, it's not about delivering the product. It's all public relations and branding. If you can get yourself written up in the *Financial Times* and juggle reports and make deals with banks so that Chris can make the numbers on the annual report shows a paper profit, you're happy. Meanwhile the things we make and the services we provide get cheaper and shoddier—until *this* happens."

"Johanna. It's true that when Naomi put me in charge of operations, I felt that increasing the amount of resources to marketing and branding and public relations would boost profit. It did."

"And now?"

Nicola ignored her. "I did it not to 'juggle numbers' but to follow your father's directive: to make the world aware of the ethical fair trade practices he believed—rightly—the public would support and *should* support."

"When you take away resources from providing a *good product* to just *posing* in front of reporters about how 'ethical' you are, the product stops being good. When it stops being good, you get *this*." Johanna slapped the paperwork before her.

Nicola rolled her eyes. "The supply chain student recites the same tired paragraphs from her college textbook. Do you have a *concrete* proposal of any *use* to make, Johanna?"

"*Look*," said Johanna, stalking over to the PowerPoint and pointing her finger at one set of numbers. "See here? The cost of our operation gathering cocoa in Ghana has risen. *Why?* It looks here like the costs of shipping have gone up, and speed of delivery have gone down. *Why?* Our distribution costs are skyrocketing. *Why?* Look at this comparison chart—our competitors are expanding their market share and ours is declining. *Why?* What are they doing right that we aren't? *We don't know*, because we don't even *have* a supply chain analyst on the company roster!"

"As I recall, the last candidate in that position walked out, leaving us stranded," said Nicola coolly.

"Why should the 'last candidate' waste her time writing analyses that the 'leadership' will only toss into the shredder?"

"*Johanna*," said Naomi. "Nicola. Stop."

Naomi placed her hands together and closed her eyes. Was she deep in thought, or in prayer? No one interrupted.

Johanna—like mother, like daughter—also closed her eyes. Before coming to the meeting, she'd first stopped at the family home to see her Father. The nurses were there, doing a home check-up, and hovered around his room like Soviet security. They would not allow Johanna to even enter his room till Naomi arrived to chaperone her. But enter she did. He'd been lying in bed, napping. She took his hand and his eyes opened dreamily. She thought he looked surprised, and almost smiled, almost as though he recognized her. But then his eyes slowly closed again. She held his hand to her cheek and could barely keep from crying.

Michael Anan had meant everything to Johanna. As a ten-year-old in Ghana she had been as free and happy as any ten-year-old could be. By fifteen, transplanted to an England she found cold, wet and strange, she'd become as wild and rude a rebel as it was possible to be. She'd plunged into teen fads, her hair became impossibly electric blue, her clothes expensive provocative tatters, her language littered with foul-mouthed American expressions. She was as passionate then as now, but with no purpose or compass or direction. She was miserably unhappy.

Then one day—the most important day, she felt, of her entire life—she had thrown a screaming tantrum at the dinner table in front of Michael, Naomi, Benjamin and Jacob and smashed a dish against the wall and ran out into the study.

Her father excused himself from the table and went to her. She was sobbing bitterly in a plush leather recliner, and expected to hear her father shout and berate her and threaten punishment. Instead he pulled over a chair and sat next to her and took her hand, just as she was taking his hand now, and said, in his rich wonderful voice, as gently as it was possible to say, "My dear little girl. What is wrong?"

She poured out everything. She was too skinny and too ugly and her legs were too fat. The boys at school laughed at her and the cold girls wouldn't let her into their cliques. British weather stank. British food stank. Everything everywhere *stank stank stank*. Most of all she had no idea where she was going or who she was or what she wanted to do.

He smiled. "Why, one day you'll be running my business. You'll be the master of this house and our offices and travel all round the world like a queen."

"I don't care about your *business*," she said, coloring the word with as much nastiness and rejection as she could.

The shock and hurt in his eyes were such that it silenced her.

Michael turned his head and looked away.

Then he looked up again and explained, slowly and carefully, as though to a child, everything. He explained what his business was, and what he was doing, and why. He explained how he carefully arranged for cocoa nuts in faraway Ghana to be picked by people whose whole lives and families depended on their company. How the nuts went from those trees and those hands to ships and to factories and to assembly lines and to designers and to packagers and to truck drivers and to stores, and finally into the hands of the customers. How everything around her and everything he and she possessed was there because he had followed a careful step-by-step path to make it so, and how he was striving with all his power to make sure that everyone along the way was treated justly and fairly so that all of them--but especially Johanna--could live well and honorably. Everything was connected, everything was interdependent, and the good of every last person involved depended on these connections--this chain.

And—she got it. *She understood!* Just as saints and scientists and mystics and revolutionaries have *Aha!* moments when everything becomes clear and all the pieces fit, so Johanna suddenly understood.

It was more than a single chain of labor and manufacture and delivery that made their own growing chocolate firm a living breathing successful business. *Everything around them* rose from such chains. Everything that she and her father and everyone else in the modern world saw or touched or owned was part of a grand network, a universe of chains, a continuum of nodes and stations and linked pathways that were responsible for proving to everyone—everything. *Everything*, the shoes on her feet, the clothes on her back, the food on the table, her bracelets, her iPod, her school, her home, *everything* was there only because these amazing and priceless *chains* of supply and manufacture were in place, and worked properly and efficiently.

For the first time, the world around her fell into place for Johanna, and suddenly made sense.

She looked at her father.

"I—understand," she said.

"Perfect!" said Michael with a laugh, and gave her a big hug. "Come on, my girl. Back to the table. Victoria Sponge Cake for desert!"

She ate the cake in a complete fog. She was transformed. Almost overnight, she went from rebel to capitalist, a capitalist with an evangelical fervor. Michael laughed about it to Naomi. "I have a disciple now!" he told the family. So he did: her hip clothing, her multicolored hair, her iPod and its millions of pop tunes, all went by the wayside. Her near-instantaneous transfiguration into a fifteen-year-old businesswoman was almost hilarious.

Eventually Michael talked her back down to earth. "If you're going to become a business woman, Johanna, you have to get an education. And a good education. And do well at school."

She got an education. A good education. And she did do well at school, jumping grades and academic hurdles like a champion mare, writing a well-reviewed journal thesis on supply chain management in her teens, graduating at the head of her class, and returning ready to enter her father's company and change the world.

Only by then her father had had his first stroke.

And instead of the Johanna leading the company, the scepter had passed to an outsider—Nicola. *Nicola*, who thought manufacture meant PR and snappy logo design and the number of hits received on social media.

Naomi opened her eyes.

"Johanna," she said.

Johanna turned to her mother.

"Do you think the business can be saved?"

"I *know* it can."

Naomi looked at her.

"In time?"

Johanna opened her mouth to answer, but stopped, lowered her eyes, and thought.

She scanned the relevant charts on the PowerPoint. Her heartbeat hammered in her chest.

Could the company be saved?

"I… think it can," she said, after a moment. "I would have to review all our business processes to be sure. Every link in the supply chain. We'd need to examine alternative processes, study the competition, look at— "

"And that would take—?"

"A year. Six months."

"We don't have months," said Nicola. "The offer needs to be responded to within thirty days."

"Weeks. Give me four weeks. *Three* weeks. I can be in Ghana tomorrow. It won't be complete, but I'm sure I can learn enough to see whether we can save the company."

Naomi sat motionless, looking into the eyes of her daughter.

"Mrs. Anan," began Nicola, "Johanna has not even been a *part* of this company for the past few—."

Naomi looked at Nicola, and then back to Johanna.

"You have four weeks," said Naomi to Johanna. "Three weeks to investigate, and a fourth to draw up and present your report."

Naomi looked around the boardroom table.

"Christopher, Nicola, Benjamin—give Johanna full access to whatever information or resources she may require.

"Nicola: if that report is negative—you are authorized to sell the business. Begin preparing the papers.

"Jacob? Accompany Johanna." She smiled at them both. "You need to see how businesses are saved."

And then, to herself, under her breath:

Or how they die.

Naomi picked up the folder Nicola had given her, and rose.

"Nicola, I'm taking this documentation with me. Johanna, give me your itinerary by tomorrow. I'm going to sit with Michael now. I don't wish to be disturbed."

She rose. So did everyone at the table.

"Children—we'll speak again."

Naomi left the room. As she did, Benjamin and Jacob immediately went to Johanna and formed a trio, bouncing ideas and comments and affectionate wisecracks off each other as they too rose and left. Chris rattled off a series of numbers that had appeared as popups on his smartphone to Nicola, who nodded without responding. Then he too gathered up his papers and, tapping into his smartphone, also left.

2

Nicola was alone. She sat down in the chief executive's chair, laced her fingers together and rested her forehead on her hands.

After a few moments, she reached down to her suitcase and put it on the table and took an cell phone out of it.

The special phone. Encrypted. Untraceable, anonymous, disposable.

It went to one and only one person.

She opened it and pressed a button.

It rang.

Once, twice. Three times.

A voice answered.

Deep, raspy, with a trace of labored breathing.

"Nicola," said the voice.

"Kwaku," said Nicola.

"Why do I have this pleasure?"

"Our Ghana operation is going to have a visitor."

A soft deep raspy laugh came from the earpiece.

"Shall I make arrangements for the visitor to be staying permanently?"

"*No*, you will *not*. *I* make the decisions," she said. "*I'm* in control here."

The laughter on the other end of the phone, Kwaku's laughter, was no longer soft, but loud and long.

Chapter Two

Accra

1

Johanna gazed out at the clouds underneath the British Airways jetliner. When she was a child her mother had taken her to Pentecostal services in Ghana and the preacher had said that Heaven would be like this—infinite clouds, infinite blue sky, beauty, timelessness—

"They have, like, bathrooms in Ghana, right?" said Jacob.

She turned in her business-class seat and made a fist. Only the fading feeling of a heavenly world kept Johanna from delivering it to Jacob's nose.

"I'm kidding! I'm kidding!"

She shook her head and looked back out through the window. Jacob was to be pitied. Or envied. Johanna wasn't sure which. It was Jacob's very first visit to Ghana. He knew a word or two of *Twi,* one of Ghana's main languages. He'd enjoyed a special dish of Jollof rice or Gari and black eye beans at father's table now and then. But often he acted as British as Boris Johnson.

Johanna had been born in Ghana. Her father had chopped cocoa nuts off trees in the fields as little Johanna watched. It was *home*.

Or it had been, once upon a time. Cold, wet, cramped, awful England had *not* been home—at first. But now she had lived as a Briton as long as she had lived as a Ghanaian. Fish and chips and Agatha Christie and *Doctor Who* had soaked into her spirit like a dye into cloth. The *first* time she returned to Ghana it had all the joy of a homecoming. But the second time she began noticing things from the outside, seen things not as a Ghanaian would see them but as—what? All she knew was that she missed fish and chips. What *Ghanaian* misses fish and chips?

Every time she returned to Ghana her pride grew. When she was born it was still emerging from colonialism and military coups. Now it was one of the most stable nations—maybe *the* most stable nation—in all western and central Africa. Its government was democratic, its economy prosperous, and best of all was an *ambition* she could feel in its people, an ambition visible in its space program. *Space exploration!* Her pride in Ghana and her people grew with each new achievement.

But *were* they her people any longer? She had lived in England and travelled in Europe so long she had become poised between the two, shifting from one to the other like a pendulum on a grandfather clock. She could see Ghana as a European would, and she could also the West as a Ghanaian would. And that was a priceless ability. Father had said it: to understand a business process that crisscrossed nations, you needed to know the cultures of those nations. She could and would see things that Jacob would miss, things that Nicola would never even notice.

But it came at a price. A homelessness. The longer she lived elsewhere, the less Ghana, for all its beauties and promise, felt like home. And yet 'elsewhere' was not home either.

She suddenly wanted to embrace Ghana, press it tightly to her and never let go. As the airliner sank into the clouds and then below them, she felt an ache, a longing to completely *belong* again. But the feeling was a recognition that perhaps she belonged no longer; not to Africa, not to Europe. To what, then?

"How about McDonalds?" said Jacob. "Ghana's *got* to have a McDonald's. *Everybody's* got a McDonalds,"

The plane began its descent into Kotoka International.

2

"Nicola?" said Chris.

Nicola looked up. She had still been sitting at the head of the boardroom table when Chris entered. Sitting so still that the lights had automatically cut themselves down to nearly darkness. They softly rose to new illumination.

"Yes, Chris?"

"I ran into your personal secretary outside. Here's a printout of your speaking engagements for the coming week. Also, your interview with the reporter from the *Financial Times*."

"Thank you," she said. "It's kind of you to deliver it."

"Sure. I'll send along some new numbers to help with the talking points."

He stood there for a moment in his fumbling, deer-in-the-headlights way.

"Nicola?"

"Yes, Chris?"

"What happens now?"

"Now?"

"I mean—to us."

She looked at him. The thick lenses, the innocent woeful expression—he looked like a Disney chipmunk with poor luck in love.

Nicola squared her shoulders. "We continue to do the very best we can for the company while we're still here."

"But how long *will* we still be here? A month? The Anan family may cash out, but the buyer isn't buying the firm from *us*. What if the new owner wants to make a clean sweep?"

As always, she masked her thoughts and feelings, but this time with a smile.

"Chris. Don't be silly. You're an effective CFO. As well as one of the most computer-proficient people in Finance I've ever worked with. Even on a personal level, the assistance you've given me recently with cryptocurrency security has been invaluable. That skill set will serve you anywhere. Any company out there would be happy to pick you up. You'd probably get a jump in salary."

"But I *like* it here," he said.

Nicola tried not to laugh. That face. She wouldn't have been surprised to see his lower lip tremble as he broke into a sob. He *was* a fine CFO—a unique one. They had an almost telepathic oneness when it came to using numbers to support market perceptions. Chris could twist and finesse data and spreadsheets till they sang. He could make dire financial situations hopeful, mediocre ones inspiring, he could reveal and conceal.

Nicola had wanted to take Chococoa from a simple chocolate supplier that did not exploit its local workers to what at times promised to become a world-class company. The next Godiva—maybe the next Starbucks. Chris was instrumental. He could see the potential behind the numbers, and give them to her to present in such a way that banks and the press could see that star potential too.

And more importantly: his data had shown Nicola all of Chococoa's weak points as well. It showed her exactly what steps she needed to take, slowly and quietly and imperceptibly, to strangle Chococoa Enterprises Limited, and starve the parasite, the *demon*, feeding on it.

The Anans would survive. Handsomely. Chris would survive too. She was glad. She genuinely liked Chris. But personally—he was a child. Unnaturally brilliant in his niche, but impulsive and emotional in life. Weak. Once she had walked into his office and seen what looked like a hundred bottles on his desk. 'Smart drugs,' he explained—Ginkgo and Ginseng, Vinpocetine and Huperzine A. All over-the-counter, he assured her! "I--I need them to focus," he'd said, as he bunglingly tried to cap them all and shove them away in his desk drawer.

Was that crutch the reason that sometimes he seemed almost staring and twitching, like a nervous colt? Nicola was concerned, but his performance was everything she could ask, and she had no wish to violate his privacy. Her own had been violated, was continually violated, and the flavor was bitter.

But—as so often—she instead tried to soothe his childishly jittery nerves, and so she consoled him now.

"If the buyer is willing to pay that much for this firm, he's going to want to hit the ground running so he can recoup some profits quickly. You don't do that by firing everyone. You're sure to be kept on. Me too—at least for a while. And who knows? Maybe Johanna will find something that can turn things around. Or maybe there'll be an unexpected surge in chocolate prices. Or maybe we can get a further extension from the banks, or find new investors. Maybe we can arrange to sell parts of the company and retain the core. Don't assume the worst," she said.

He nodded, pacified.

"Go. Get to work."

He nodded again, smiled, placed the printouts in front of her, and left.

Nicola took a deep breath, and proceeded to assume the worst.

Yes, Chris would survive.

Would *she?*

Would she even be alive in a month's time?

Kwaku would not smile, nod, and let her prance out to work on her resume. Kwaku would leave her hanging from one of the lampposts outside by her guts.

Unless *Kwaku* was the buyer. Was that it? Was that it? Was he finally making his move to take over the company entirely?

Then there wouldn't even be the illusion of any kind of parity between them. He would snap his fingers, and she would execute his whims. Or die.

Quiet, she said to her own thoughts. *You've been preparing for this day for a long time. You have a plan. A logical rational plan. Be ready. Be ready to execute it. Deliberately. Coldly.*

She closed her eyes again, focusing on her breathing, on calm, on control.

And then, instead, she exploded, and with a cry Nicola savagely swept the printouts from the desk.

How? How did I let it all go this far?

The sheets flew into the air and fluttered down like gulls' wings.

3

Streaming along with the Kotoka International airport crowds, Jacob and Johanna saw a large blue sign ahead.

"*Akwaaba!*" it said. "Welcome to Ghana."

A guide wearing a blindingly white shirt a pale beige suit stood underneath, holding up another sign, with the Anan name on it. His eyes scanned the rolling crowd.

"Miss Anan? Miss Anan?" he cried.

She called out. "Here!"

He grinned. "Welcome! Come, follow me, please."

Johanna and Jacob followed him through the jostling crowd and stepped outside. Sleek two-seater motorcycles with painted flames on the gas tanks waited for them. The drivers revved the engines.

"Motorcycles?" said Jacob. "*Motorcycles?*"

"You were expecting a limousine?"

"Well—yes."

"Spoiled brat."

"But I've never ridden a motorcycle!"

"Those two are doing the driving. We're just sitting behind them, hanging on. And you'd better hang on tight."

"But—"

"Trust me. You want to get through Accra traffic? A car is the *last* thing you want to drive."

The smaller of the motorcyclists slid off, zipped down a tight leather jacket, and removed a futuristic shell of a helmet. Dreadlocks spilled out, framing the face of a woman that made Jacob's jaw drop. It was his turn to experience Heaven now.

"Boy. You come here," she said.

Jacob made a gurgling sound.

"Here. Now." She slapped the seat behind her.

Johanna looked at her brother and smiled wickedly. "Well? Put your arms around her waist, Romeo, and hold on tight. Think you can manage that?"

"Now!" barked the girl.

Johanna secured her briefcase, overnight bag, and Jacob's backpack on the first motorcycle. She knew the routine. She donned the extra helmet and mounted the seat like a rodeo cowboy.

"Jacob, have you got your helmet on? Are you secure?" said Johanna.

"Y-yes," he said, his forearms tightly wrapping his driver's Olympic midriff.

Johanna looked up. The Ghanaian skies were already darkening into evening.

She nodded to her driver.

Both machines tore off into Accra traffic, with a scream from Jacob and a blistering roar.

4

"Graham," said Benjamin. "Got a minute?"

"Yeah," said Charles Graham, the Operations head of the Chococoa manufacturing facilities at Derby. He was a

Scot who had worked in America for thirty years, and it had left its mark. Competent fellow, but for some reason he always made Benjamin think of cheeseburgers.

"I have been commissioned to inspect the supply chain of our operations at the Derby plant."

"You? You're a lawyer, ain't you?"

Ain't. Benjamin shuddered.

"I am indeed a solicitor, Graham. Nonetheless that is my commission. Can you help me facilitate it?"

"Well—yeah, sure. Basically you want to do a tour, right?"

"Yes. I'd like to be walked through each link or node or section—whatever you call it—of our chocolate manufacturing process. I'd also like someone familiar with all the steps, or those individuals most familiar with each of the steps, to accompany me and answer any questions I may ask."

"No offense, Mr. Benjamin, but do you *know* what questions to ask?"

"No offense taken, Graham. I'm doing so not out of personal curiosity. Johanna, my sister, plans to undertake a more thorough review in a week or so personally. She asked me to lay the groundwork, and provide her with some information that she needs while she's out of the country. She'll tell me what to look for and I'll report back till she arrives next week to review things in person."

"Johanna's back?" said Graham. A smile broke across his otherwise craggy features like early sunlight. Benjamin more than understood, and smiled back. He was buoyant. He loved Johanna. She made life fun. She was scrappy and contentious and argumentative. A natural solicitor! Except that she got things working, whereas a solicitor's task was more often a matter of dragging things out. Nicola had given Chococoa three to six months. He snorted. If he couldn't drag that out past a year he didn't deserve to see an episode of *Rumpole* ever again!

He and Johanna had taken very different paths. It had

to do with Great Britain, he supposed. They were roughly the same age when they arrived and Johanna found it all strange and alien. She came around to savoring its virtues, but slowly. Benjamin loved everything about England from the very beginning, from Big Ben to Earl Grey to red double-decker buses to pop bands.

Most of all, even more than he loved the English language, he loved *Rumpole Of The Bailey*. Johanna was always a doer, but Benjamin was a reader, his young nose always buried in a book. Even as a boy in Ghana he devoured detective novels. He went through Perry Mason mysteries the way other Ghanaian children went through boiled plantains.

Like Johanna, he too had had a transformative moment: watching *Rumpole* for the first time. That, he knew instantly, was what he wanted to be: supremely articulate, brilliant, tearing the mask off Evil while those astounded buffoons, the Judges, sputtered and gasped. The reality of English Law was not quite like that, of course, but even as a boy he would rehearse Rumpole's speeches before the court in front of his delighted father and Naomi, and glory in their applause.

It helped that he really *was* articulate and brilliant. His parents spared no expense on an education that honed his gifts, and the investment was well spent: in time Benjamin formed a law office all his own, with Chococoa its chief client, and by no means its most prominent one. No firm could have a more active or protective solicitor.

And yet—he had to admit that he knew little enough of the actual operations of the company that he legally secured and defended. Perhaps there was no longer any need to do so. It was strange to think that in a month he might be drawing up and reviewing a contract for the sale of Chococoa.

And yet, would that really be so bad? He had mixed feelings. Father, sadly, would not miss the company, not in his current condition. Naomi had her academics and Father to take care of. The sale and departure of Chococoa would hurt his practice, but not fatally—assuming the new owners *did* take Chococoa to another firm.

On the other hand, Naomi said there were millions to be dispensed to the family in the event of a sale. A few million pounds... hmm—perhaps the time had come to retire to Venice and work on that John Grisham mystery novel he had been planning to write since forever.

He shook his head. No: there was a worse scenario: the buyer might change his mind and pull out, and the declining business hang on till it collapsed under the weight of its own bank debt and inefficiency.

Then the family would have nothing, their employees might be thrown to the four winds, and the firm would be cannibalized by corporate pirates here and child trafficking competitors in Ghana.

His shoulders straightened. No, he would not allow that. He would *not*. He would help Johanna locate the cancer draining the life from the company. Who knows? Perhaps in helping Johanna he *was* tearing the mask off Evil. Or at least keeping it at bay.

The feeling filled him with joy.

"Let's work out that itinerary in detail, Graham."

"You got it, Boss."

5

The motorcycles roared, twisted, pitched, veered at the last minute; they slid through the cramped disorderly Accra traffic like blood corpuscles sliding through networks of throbbing veins. Cars, trucks, bicycles, military vehicles, taxis, *tro-tros* with directors shouting directions, ancient imported Soviet Zils from the time of Nkrumah, all of them bustling along in a chaotic glut. It took the reflexes of a panther to slip rapidly through. And they slid through *more* than rapidly: they flew like hawks, twisted like snakes. Time and again behind her Johanna heard a blood-curdling shriek from Jacob. But not a crash.

She had asked for the best, and gotten them. The motorcyclists stopped for nothing, not traffic lights, not police, not pedestrians. In short, they drove like most Accra drivers. But at light speed, and without a single accident. Johanna's driver was so good and so fast that he even managed to look behind him now and again. Suspiciously, she thought. Why?

But his head snapped back into the ongoing wind as they forded the honking chaos and exhaust fumes of Ring Road Central and the Ako Adjei Interchange.

As they dove into the spaghetti-like convolutions of Kwame Nkrumah Circle, another humming motorcycle drew alongside Johanna's, paralleling its motions perfectly. The space between them seemed less than the space of a human hair.

She looked at the rider alongside her. He was masked against the choking exhaust fumes just as she was, but she felt his cold dark eyes pass over her. *Stare*, knowingly.

Her driver pressed the pedal harder. She felt as though both of them were about to break the sound barrier.

The rider slammed into them!

She gasped. The entire frame of their motorcycle wobbled and groaned as her driver swore hard and struggled for control. Through the corner of her eye she saw the other rider flicker away into traffic elsewhere as her own driver's shoulders heaved, trying to twist the handlebars back into place as the motorcycle's exhaust, now at an angle, scraped across a taxi's side to their left, spitting sparks.

She shut her eyes, bracing for impact, prayed—

And suddenly, magically, everything righted itself.

She felt her driver inhale, exhale, curse, inhale exhale.

They slid forward again like a dazzling snake through grass.

6

Nicola Cavalcanti first met Michael Anan in a class she regularly gave at the London Business School. The class was always in danger of being cancelled, for she was not a popular lecturer. As classes began, half the students would be boys who followed her down the streets and corridors because of her looks. As classes progressed, her cold manner and brutally cutting remarks to attendees who only took the class to admire her drove them away. The handful of remaining students were enraptured by what she had to say, not how she looked. And she had a good deal to say.

Beauty meant nothing to Nicola Cavalcanti. Her parents died in a car crash when she was an infant. She was raised as a ward of the State, and never adopted. It was her looks—she ballooned early on and was grossly fat from her very first days of school. As she grew older, pimples and acne crossed her face like a volcanic pinkish landscape. She stuttered, she lisped. The staff neglected her, and she neglected herself. Her days were a skein of humiliation, wretchedness, self-pity and an overwhelming *determination* to escape.

But the bars would not open. Till, after a late puberty, somehow the trigger rush of hormones changed everything: her skin cleared, her fat melted away, she went from being short and bulky to tall and slim, supermodel-like. Even her voice changed from a jittery stutter to a smooth deep contralto. Boys began to accumulate around her like magnetic filings. Finally there were compliments, invitations, offers.

But she knew what they all wanted, and she despised them all for it. She was who she was. She always had been who she was. All that had changed was her appearance. Now people that would otherwise have ignored or overlooked or insulted her brutally were dazzled. But not by *her*. By her looks. Her shell. Nicola's looks might have gone from one extreme to the other, but looks—

horrible or lovely—were just a mask.

And what they masked in Nicola's case was a cool formidable intelligence. She had analyzed her situation; seen its implications. The reaction to her looks had taught her to see the impact of pure appearance on people, how easily it could manipulate their responses and their actions.

She told herself that she had been given a gift: that she, uniquely, because of how she had been treated by others, could put appearance aside and see through it to the person or the reality underneath. She saw and understood how easily appearances could manipulate a person.

Cold treatment had left her cold, but not only cold: also analytical. It wasn't enough to resent her suffering: She wanted to understand people, why they misjudged, why they suffered, why they did the cruel and foolish things they did.

And she could use her newfound beauty, her intelligence, to help her find out. When the time came for University, those looks combined with her stellar scores opened virtually all doors. She opted for Psychology, taking degrees at an accelerated pace, writing and publishing papers on how appearance manipulated behavior. Businesses took note, and she began making presentations about presentation, personal and corporate. Eventually she formed a startup all on her own giving high-ticket seminars on psychology and consumer behavior.

But she continued her University connection, and when Michael Anan approached her after class one evening, after silently attending several of her classes on psychology and marketing, she was taken with him. His English was quirky and he had strong but not classically handsome features. But his strong dark face seemed *focused*, and focused on more than just her transitory looks. Externals meant nothing to Nicola, and she sensed a kindred spirit. But what mattered most of all was that he asked her a question that stuck her like a thorn.

"Can your psychology and your marketing help people to do good?"

"How do you mean?"

"I have a business. A chocolate business. Other companies do the same business. But they are larger than my business. Because they use slaves. Child slaves. They pay them next to nothing, and treat them how they like. The cost savings let them sell chocolate cheap, and make the companies strong and rich. Stronger and richer than mine.

"But," he said. "I think the hearts of most people are *good*. I think people will be glad to spend more, a little more, if they know what they are buying is not—dirty. If they know their money comes from a source that treats the people that make it with justice and dignity."

Justice and dignity. She thought of her childhood, with its endless injustices, its petty indignities. How little justice and dignity there is in this world, she thought.

Nicola prided herself on being able to see through people, *into* people. She looked at Michael Anan. And she saw into him. Yes, he believed what he was saying. Every word. She loved him for what he was saying. She closed her eyes, collected herself.

"What you are saying is: is it possible to create a marketing plan that will allow a business to thrive against competition despite higher production costs by specifically making an ethical appeal to the market?"

He scratched his head. "Yes."

"Yes," she said. "It is."

She assigned him additional reading. Philip Kotler and Nancy R. Lee's *Social Marketing*.

He smiled, a grand, wonderful smile. He thanked her.

When he reached the door, she said, "Mr. Anan."

"Yes?"

"What's the name of your company."

"Chococoa," he said with visible pride.

She made a note.

"Will you be available for coffee next week? I may have a few ideas to share."

7

The motorcycles pulled into the down ramp of an abstract glassy building that could have been either a massive garage or a corporate research facility. Neither parked: Johanna's driver pressed a clicker on his handlebars and slowed down as sliding metal doors opened toward the far end. Both vehicles pulled in and the doors closed behind them.

Jacob clambered off his motorcycle and pulled off his helmet.

"Johanna, what the *hell!*"

The floor shook and rose.

They were in an elevator.

Jacob looked around, and turned back to Johanna.

"Are you all *right?*" he said.

"That man hit us deliberately," she said to her driver, who was removing his helmet. He was in his forties, and had a large strong unshaven face.

He nodded. In *Twi*, he added, "He was following us." He turned his head, thinking.

"Well, report him!" sputtered Jacob.

The girl driver laughed.

"What happened out there?" said Johanna to the driver.

"He was playing," said Johanna's driver. "A *hard* hard turn just then? We would be in the hospital. Maybe in the graveyard. That was a tap."

"A warning?" she said.

He shrugged. "Maybe. Maybe just someone on drugs."

"Someone on drugs alert enough to follow us?"

The man smiled crookedly. No, he didn't think so

either.

The doors opened. Johanna could see the darkening evening sky. The crystalline Ghanaian stars. They were on the roof.

"Jacob, get our stuff out there," she said, tossing him his backpack and her overnight bag.

"We're staying on the *roof?*"

"Just go," she said. She looked at the scratches on the motorcycle. "We'll pay for any damages," she said to her driver.

"Yes, you will," he said with a smile. "And extra for the drive back." He took out a business card and a short pencil and wrote down the license plate number of the motorcycle that hit them. "Probably stolen. But you never know."

She took it.

"Thank you," she said, and took her briefcase and went out onto the roof.

Jacob was standing there, under the ever more starry sky, looking at a helicopter that was repeatedly trying to start its engine.

"A *helicopter?* First motorbikes and now a *helicopter?*"

"Just get in."

"Just tell me why!"

"It's rainy season."

"So?"

"So I want to see the fields. Talk to the workers. Look at the cocoa trees. The rain is falling over the roads that take us there. The last time I drove through those roads in rainy season the entire car went underwater. This will take us right over everything."

Jacob opened his mouth to protest again, but nodded. That made sense.

Johanna checked her smartphone for messages. The two motorcyclists began suiting up.

Jacob asked Johanna for a spare business card and a pencil. She was never without either. He wrote something down on the card and ran over and gave it to his motorcycle driver, the dreadlocked girl, who was yawning and stretching, and gave it a puzzled look.

Jacob turned, and went to the platform where the helicopter, roaring, had finally started up.

He threw in his backpack and waved Johanna in. "Come on."

Johanna shut off her phone and joined him.

The two of them pulled over their seatbelts and secured themselves as the pilot watched and double-checked, and finally buckled himself in as well.

He looked in the mirror at Johanna.

Johanna nodded.

The helicopter lifted off the platform.

"What was that all about?" shouted Johanna above the din.

"What?"

"The card."

"What?"

"The card. Just now. You wrote something down. What did you write down?"

"Nothing," he said.

"What—"

But by then it was impossible to hear anything.

The elevator doors opened on basement floor. The driver revved his engine and looked over the side of his vehicle again, running his fingers along the scratch. The girl on the motorcycle pulled her futuristic helmet over her dreadlocks and zipped up her leather jacket.

She reached into her pocket and looked at the back of the business card the young man had given her.

It had a phone number written on it, along with the words "Thanks" and a drawing of a heart with an arrow through it.

She threw her head back and laughed and tossed the card in the air as the two of them roared away.

8

The helicopter soared high over the city of Accra, its streets, its buildings, its millions of people. Darkest Africa? At night the city of Accra was a multi-faceted jewel, casting flashes and dazzles of brilliance and neon below that rivaled the light of the stars above. Jacob stared, amazed, at the Nkrumah Memorial, Osu Castle, the Makola bazaar, Independence Arch, the seafront beaches, as the urban glitter and bustle turned into quiet outer boroughs, then finally into swathes of dark forests. Johanna failed to notice. Her eyes were going over the reports that had been waiting for her in the helicopter. You could trace a supply chain out physically, following each link directly by eye, and she would shortly do just that. But there were other aspects of the process that only numbers and technical assessments could reveal. She plunged into them obsessively.

The data was yet another forest; and somewhere among the wilderness of data lay the key to the survival of the business.

But once, when her head turned, she saw Jacob staring wide-eyed out at the forests, now a vast murmuring starlit sea of emerald, waving below them in the night. That expression on his face. He was astonished. Exalted. It pleased her, and touched her.

Ghana—Ghana in all its glory. Our land, our people, the home of our ancestors.

Our home, my brother.

Chapter Three

Chains

1

"We're supposed to spend the night *here?*" said Jacob.

"You were expecting a Jacuzzi?" said Johanna

"Well—yeah. There's, like, not even a PlayStation!"

Johanna rolled her eyes.

They were in one of several processing warehouses owned by Chococoa Incorporated, Ghana Division. The warehouse was two stories high and seemed about half the size of a soccer field. The walls were metal the floor concrete; everything was there for a reason, and not a cent had been spent making it decorative. In places, hundreds of fat jute bags sat stacked almost to the ceiling. Other areas hosted long silvery humming ramps that, even now, automatically sifted and sorted cocoa beans. A few dozen night workers ran around performing maintenance, and large unmanned forklift trucks sat silent, like sleeping robots in Transformer movies.

Johanna had seen it all before; Jacob stared wide-eyed around himself as the two walked to a corner far from the ramps and the work areas. There, next to the manager's office, was a small room reserved for conferences and meetings. It included foldable cots stored away in the closet for visitors or a manager in need of a quick nap.

Ten hours ago the plant manager got a phone call informing him that two members of the Anan Family itself would be dropping in for a tour and an inspection. Six hours ago the call came from Johanna Anan herself, informing him that she wanted to start reviewing their reports and records immediately upon arrival, and to stay at the warehouse throughout their visit.

This particular building bordered on the property of one of the largest cocoa farmers working in association with Chococoa. It was night, but come morning you could walk out and in a few minutes you would see and could talk to people harvesting cocoa beans directly. That was exactly what Johanna wanted, and she didn't want to waste time driving to and from a comfortable hotel to do it.

They had been greeted upon arrival by the warehouse manager, who was a man in his sixties with grizzled white hair, a wide smile, and a gap between his two front teeth. He had pulled up in a jeep, had been promoted to his job only recently, and looked as though he had just been pulled out of bed. He seemed both confused and taken aback when Johanna, a girl half his age, and Jacob, a boy ten years younger, dropped out of the night sky in the middle of the parking lot where tomorrow trucks taking cocoa beans to Tama Harbor were lined up and arranged.

The two visitors got out and brushed off the dust motes kicked around by the still slowly whirling rotors flickering in the manager's headlights.

"Have you got all the paperwork and other records together?" Johanna had shouted over the propeller racket. She turned and pulled her suitcases out of the helicopter.

"Yes, Miss Anan," he had said. "In the conference room. Come. Sit."

"We'll walk. I'll meet you there."

She wanted to point things out to Jacob—the efficiency of the truck arrangements, the on-site garage, the security cameras that reduced pilfering and provided a legal record in case of accidents. All the small coordinated details that made a warehouse work smoothly and profitably, as opposed to being a costly ongoing confusion.

They entered the conference room. It had the no-nonsense utilitarian look of an Army field cafeteria, but everything was laid out on the tables as instructed. She informed the new manager that they'd be going over the papers and computer data till late at night. Were the sleeping arrangements ready? The manager walked to a door in the far right and rolled out two folded sleeping cots with pillows.

Unasked, he also rolled out a small portable refrigerator and a coffee machine.

"There are other supplies in that door over there," he said to Jacob. "Forks, knives, bandages, additional computers, chargers. Behind that door there is a shower and a sink and bidet."

Johanna was already plugging in.

"Excellent," she said. "Everything I requested, as requested." She made a note of his name. Good work deserved to be acknowledged. "You'll be available in a few hours?'

"When the sun is up," he said. "Yes."

"Be here at 7 AM," she said. "*Exactly* at 7 AM."

The manager had served in the Ghanaian armed forces at one time, and his arm wanted to give a crisp salute. But he restrained himself.

Johanna felt the emphasis was needed. Clock time and Ghana time were not always perfectly aligned. Sometimes that was a good thing. The people they employed got the job done. If it took more time, they didn't count the minutes. In England, one second of unpaid work over the clock and Jeremy Corbyn would be storming Buckingham Palace. On the other hand, 'now' in Ghana had a way of being understood as 'maybe later.' Time for many Ghanaians was like an Italian coffee break: the hours stretched out in ways only Albert Einstein could fathom.

But this manager had everything set up perfectly and was waiting on the dot as they arrived. He got it. Nothing more needed to be said. She turned and stared into her computer screen, her fingers flying.

The manager looked at Jacob. Jacob shrugged. He had no idea what she would do or say next either.

The manager looked at them both, nodded to both, and said, "Good night, young sir. Good night, Miss Anan." And left.

Outside, he looked up into Ghana's night sky. Night was clear and black. The stars twinkled so!

He removed his smartphone and pressed an encrypted number.

"Mr. Kwaku? They have arrived, sir. No, they do not appear to be injured. Yes, the recording devices are in operation. Yes, sir. I will, sir."

The call cut out.

Poor boy, thought the manager, thinking of how Jacob too had looked amazed up at the same lovely stars. *Poor little girl.*

2

Jacob unpacked.

"You can stick your nose in a computer at a top-rated hotel too, you know," said Jacob.

"And waste hours trying to get here once I'm off the computer? No thank you. Night time is quiet, and less busy, and I can look over actual field reports, not data entries based on them."

"You think there are discrepancies?"

"There are always discrepancies. The question is, are they trivial, or are they serious?"

"Can I help?"

"Yes. Get me a cup of coffee. Then leave me alone and let me work in peace."

Jacob's eyes flashed.

"Hey. Cut back on that attitude, Jo. I'm here for a *reason*, you know? I'm supposed to *learn*. You're supposed to show me how to save a company. *Our* company. Is this how you do it? By dropping in out of nowhere and getting the warehouse manager to point me to the toilet? What are you doing over there anyway?"

Johanna looked up.

She began to snap back an answer, but stopped. Her expression changed.

"You're right," she said. "I apologize."

Jacob's mouth fell open. "Are you kidding me?"

She stared into his eyes. "We're going to survive, Jacob. Chococoa is going to *survive* and *prosper*. One day you'll be doing what I'm doing. Who knows? One day you may be running the company."

She jerked her head at one of the folding chairs.

"Pull up a seat."

3

Naomi sat by Michael Anan's bedside. As she had throughout his entire convalescence, she gave a full report on the discussion in the boardroom. She tried to make it as clear and objective as possible.

Michael's head lay back on the down pillow.

The bed was a Hästens, the bed of choice for Swedish royalty, fully bespoke and hand-made. *Royalty*—what could be more appropriate. Royalty was always what she thought of when she thought of Michael. What she thought from the very first.

His eyes were closed, as though in thought. She touched his hair.

"And so Johanna is in Ghana now," she concluded. "And she's brought Jacob along too. Double the trouble, I'm sure!"

Michael's lips looked almost as though he was smiling.

4

Jacob adjusted his chair. Johanna sat at what looked like an industrial picnic table staring into her Macintosh Pro. Her fingers danced over the keys.

"Simulation modeling—" began Johanna.

"And that is—?"

"No, forget simulation modeling for now. Basics first. A supply chain," began Johanna, now in lecture mode, "is the discrete series of behaviors and events that occur as a product goes from its initial starting point to its final sale to the customer."

"In English, please?"

She waved a hand at a few jute bags stuffed with cocoa beans in the corner.

"Here's the big picture. Take chocolate. Someone has to pick the beans. Someone has to sort out the bad ones from the good ones and put the good ones into sacks like those over there for shipping. Someone has to ship them. Someone has to take the bags of beans to the factory. Once there, someone has to add milk to make the milk chocolate that you buy. Someone has to package it. Someone has to take the packaged chocolate to the chocolate stores. That's it, start to finish. Got it now, Jacob?"

"Got it."

"No, you're an idiot. You don't get it. Look closer. *Think.* Before anyone can pick anything, someone has to plant the trees that grow the cocoa beans. Before they're planted, the soil needs to be examined to see whether the seeds can grow there. The weather conditions need to be studied, to see if cold snaps will freeze the seeds, to see if rains will flood the soil, to see if the temperature and moisture encourages insects that chew away the seeds, the beans, the trees. Did you know that 30% of world cocoa production is lost to pests or diseases?"

"No."

"Well, now you do. Thirty percent is lost—" she tapped the screen of her Mac—"*unless* you can figure out what causes that loss, and intervene effectively. Pick the right seeds, the right soil, get the right conditions set up properly *first*, and your productivity and profit take off."

" 'Victorious warriors win first and then go to war, while defeated warriors go to war first and then seek to win'," said Jacob.

Johanna looked up, surprised. "You know Sun Tzu?" she said.

"It was a subtitle in a ninja movie. So what's all this have to do with stimulation?"

"*Sim*ulation. Simulation modeling. This custom software here allows me to build a model of the entire supply chain from start to end. At each stage in the process it prompts me with questions that I answer till I can provide a complete description of what's happening at each point in the process. There's a section where I can add information that it doesn't ask, but should, and when I see that, I modify the simulation so I can gather even more information and do it better every time. And you know what happens when I get all the relevant information together?"

"What?"

"I see how *it all works*. Or where it doesn't work, and needs fixing or improvement. I see how it hangs together. I see where we're strong, and where we're weak. I not only see what's going on, I can compare it to other models. Competing models. I'm able to see whether what we're doing is as good, or better, or worse than competitors. I can see if we're reaching competitive benchmarks or milestones. I can make small changes in the data and see what *could* happen if we try something differently. What if we *don't* use pesticides at all? Well?"

Jacob shrugged. "Beats me. More bugs eat the cocoa beans and we lose money, I guess."

"The first part of that is correct. We have fewer beans. But what if we sell what remains to the market as pesticide-free and organic, and charge more? Jacob?"

"Well… if you charge so *much* more that it makes up for the beans you lose, I guess you make more money. If enough people buy it."

"Correct. Very good. You know what GMO's are?"

"Genetically modified foods."

"Yes. Larger, longer lasting, tastier, more disease-resistant. Say we decide to grow GMO strains. How much more will we produce if the beans are larger? If the ripeness and picking season is longer. If fewer beans are diseased?"

"How much *less* do we sell if people who hate GMO's don't buy it?"

"Brilliantly put."

Johanna tapped the screen.

"With enough information," she said, "with the *right* information, you can make a reasonable prediction. You input data that shows, say, how GMO's have impacted *other* chocolate products sales. Then you balance that against the greater supply you generate. Do the numbers work out? If they work out, it may be worth doing."

"So, basically, with this sim here you get a clear picture of what's going on—"

"Crystal clear."

"And a clear picture of what's *going* to happen if we make changes."

"Prediction's a little trickier than analysis. Let's say simulation modeling will help you get the best predictions you *can* get, if your input is correct. You're also able to see the impact on other things, like sustainability."

"What's that?

"Lord. What do they teach you at school?"

"Genderfluid sensitivity. And soccer."

Johanna looked up towards the ceiling. "How long, O Lord?" she mumbled.

"Come on, tell me."

"Look. Say Chococoa finds a pesticide that repels the insects that attack our cocoa beans. The insects leave the beans alone. That's *good*, right?"

"Right."

"But the insects are still hungry. What are they going to eat now?"

"Fish and chips?"

"They start eating the leaves off the trees. What happens then?"

"No leaves?"

"No leaves. So some of the trees die, or maybe they become diseased, because the leaves supplied chemicals needed for them to thrive. Or maybe the extra sunlight coming through overheats the cocoa pods, and the cocoa beans come out malformed or funny-tasting, and we can't use them. Or maybe there's so much sun that it gives the workers in the field sunstroke, and their families sue. Was using that pesticide a good idea?"

"No."

"No. Well, Jacob, *this*," she said, pointing to her laptop screen, "this simulation, this model, *if* you set it up right, let's us see what's happening if and as we implement that. It lets us see what's happening *right* now, but it also helps us forecast what *may* happen if the effects are negative, and what the profit margins could be if the effects are positive. It lets us experiment on screen, but keeps the experiment from blowing up in our faces in real life."

"So if you find out that the only way to save the company is to cut everyone's salary by 2%—"

"Or to cut spending on marketing by 2%. Or to buy new processors that sort cocoa beans 20% faster and more efficiently. Or to—"

"—then that's the decision you make. Huh!" he said,

walking around and looking at the screen. "You know, this would make a pretty cool video game. Super Mario Supply Chain Brothers! You just need a couple of cool icons."

Johanna thought of responding with a smart crack, but instead pulled up a pop-up box and made a note. *Game models for training?*

Maybe Jacob was on to something.

5

Kwaku turned down the button that controlled the volume. He could watch the full recording of Johanna and her brother Jacob later. The microphones and surveillance cameras would start automatically whenever either of them moved or made a sound.

He touched another control on the remote. He sat in one of the several homes he owned in hard-to-penetrate forest areas outside Accra. A half dozen men armed with machine guns strode around outside. They appeared on screen in separate rectangles on the HDTV. He watched them casually, and pressed another button. A series of infographic pop-ups of radio-activated mines and booby traps and getaway routes succeeded one another on screen.

Nothing was happening. Good. He wished to reflect.

The house itself was an essay in geometrical Swedish Modern. Nothing less Ghanaian could be imagined. He made it so out of pure whim. He did it as he did many things—purely because he could. He took a small Moleskin notebook out of the pocket of his smoking jacket and made a few notes. The chat between Jacob and Johanna had sparked a few thoughts. Looking in on Chococoa always did.

Hm. Had he really been giving enough attention to developing new and more addictive drugs? Cocaine and heroin were all well and good, but opioids were a whole new growing market in North America. Time to import? And those young people of his, selling drugs on the street—who knows, maybe a video game, where the plucky young dealer avoids every trap of the police, might train them better than shouting and threats.

Innovate, Mr. Kwaku, innovate! You're a businessman, remember?

Chococoa. It had taught him so much. Observing its operations, he felt at times like the true father of the child of another man. He could claim no credit, but he'd watched it grow with pride, and helped it along invisibly. Seeing it flourish had taught him much.

Observing Chococoa really was the turning point. His rise to the middle levels of the drug industry in Ghana had been meteoric, but he never began to even approach the top until he stopped looking at his activities in terms of mere crime and started looking at it in terms of business operations. Supply, demand, recruitment, logistics. Businesses were unique, but the principles were universal.

Perhaps he would find a simulation modeler of his own—one with family members, so as to ensure secrecy and compliance. After all, what was his *own* business but a commercial supply chain with unique challenges? The component elements of drugs had to be grown, delivered to a place of processing, converted to chemicals, and properly mixed. They needed to meet certain quality levels, they needed trustworthy distributors, transactions needed to be correctly recorded. The chain he managed operated in the shadows, but even so it could be mapped and rendered as a simulation and in that way improved and developed.

Perhaps Johanna could be the map-maker…

But unfortunately she seemed strong-willed. Very strong-willed. Of course no one was strong-willed once they set that will against Kwaku's. There was no one Kwaku could not break. But putting the shattered pulverized little pieces back together so they operated properly—that was not always possible.

No, better to let her finish her study of Chococoa before making any decisions. He wanted to see what she came up with. There were lessons to be learned as he followed her little investigation. He could decide what to do with her, if anything, later.

Now *Nicola* had taught him very different lessons—lessons in presentation, and perception. Dear Nicola, he thought, smiling. Before Nicola, he had been a smart, if strange and freakishly disfigured, thug. After Nicola, like Nicola, he had become a Brand. A *presence*.

Nicola had taught him the value of packaging. Kwaku's skin was very dark, almost blue-black. His clothing had been plain. He cared nothing for clothes, decorations, frills. One look at the remains of his face, he thought, and who would notice what he was wearing? Owing to Nicola he had grasped the value of *style*. As his star rose even higher, he took to wearing expensive, blindingly all-white suits and gloves. His near-sighted eyes were brown, and (unexpectedly, in the carnage of the rest of his face) gentle islands of deceptive kindness.

No longer: he never appeared to anyone anymore without custom-designed contact lenses that were a large brilliant electric blue with pinprick pupils, the edges marred with bleeding flaws of bright aortal red. The eyes were riveting now, frightening—insane. Occasionally he would replace them with golden long-slit *cats-eye* contacts. The terror *those* stares inspired was hilarious to behold. His men passed rumors along that he was possessed by demons. Rumors that he *was* a demon. He chuckled. After a while they started to believe it themselves.

Once, shortly after reading an article of Nicola's in *Business Insider*, he had a meeting with a competitor. A larger, stronger competitor, whom he wished to absorb. They were to meet in a room in Accra behind a trendy cafe. Prior to the meeting he went to the lavatory, taking along his briefcase. In it was a chicken whose neck he had broken before arriving. He cut open its throat and belly over the sink, splashed the blood all over his face and the brilliance of his white suit, and flushed the chicken bits down the toilet.

He still laughed remembering the looks on the faces of the other drug lord and his men, and even of his own men, as he entered, wearing dark sunglasses. He sat himself at the table, noted a slice of some organ or other on his lapel, flicked it away, and then slowly removed his dark sunglasses and looked into the eyes of the other man—now one of his lesser lieutenants—and unleashed his cat's-eye *stare.*

He could smell the urine staining the other's pants. Truly, marketing was the key to sales.

6

The first month of Nicola's appointment as Director of Marketing and Public Relations at Chococoa was a tsunami of interviews, appearances, accolades. She directed her staff to contact not just everyone of note in the chocolate and confectionary industry, but everyone in the news media generally, as well as politicians, social activists, churches, vegan film stars, social media celebrities, environmentalists. Each received a clear, tightly focused message: Chococoa was only incidentally the producer of the finest chocolate in the world. Principally it was the way one Ghanaian, Michael Anan, was lifting his fellow countrymen out of poverty, feeding and educating children, empowering women, and fighting child trafficking and human exploitation. When called or interviewed, Nicola barely mentioned chocolate at all: she spoke of Michael forging a new people-centered grass-roots capitalism, building a revolutionary market-driven African model of spreading and redistributing wealth.

The amazing thing about it was that it was not

untrue. The first rule of marketing, Nicola knew, was never to lie. True, one didn't have to give the media *all* the information one had, particularly if it might hurt the marketing message; but what one did say had to be the absolute truth.

In this case it was. Yes, it had had to evolve to that point. In the beginning, the company Michael founded operated the way all the other companies operated. Their model worked, so he copied it till his was stable too.

But then he began to innovate. He took his inspiration from Henry Ford: the idea that better-paid, better-treated, better-educated employees did better work, and produced a better product. Chococoa paid workers more, so as to attract better workers. They helped to provide medical care and Day Care, they helped young workers get free training and supported them if they sought higher education, they gave pregnant women paid leave and new parents time with their newborn children. Management sought input from workers at every level, and rewarded employees at any level who came up with ideas for improving efficiency and increasing profitability. Workers came from all over Ghana to compete to work for Chococoa, and those who did so successfully were an elite—loyal, hard-working, and evangelical. Slowly, almost inadvertently, Chococoa became a *brand*, a name people thought of when they thought of the best of Ghana. Quality improved. Awards were won. Productivity rose.

But profit—when there was profit—was razor-thin. Like most startups, Chococoa started deeply in debt to investors and banks, flirting with bankruptcy on a daily basis. And while Michael's philosophy of employee cultivation was producing a happier, more loyal, more competent and productive workforce, and in turn a superior product, sales were not rising at the same rate as expenses. Unless things changed, the business would fail. And the cumulative direction of failure was so strong that it seemed only a miracle could save Chococoa.

Nicola was the miracle. He had met her in London, and she changed nothing about Michael's policies, nor had she thoroughly mastered the operational processes of the business itself. But she was a psychologist, she knew the *mind*, and in particular her specialty: the mind of the market. She ran focus groups and ordered **in-depth** questionnaires and observed videos of consumer behavior in shops, but they all confirmed Michael Anan's key insight: people ate sweets because they wanted to feel good. They didn't feel good if they thought the people making their sweets were being mistreated and exploited and suffered in poverty. Nicola ran with it: she went to every platform she could and tore the cover off the shabby practices of (tactfully unnamed) other companies, and pointed to Chococoa as the shining counterexample, the way forward for Africa, for labour, for all businesses everywhere.

The press loved it. The media loved *her*. Nicola's look alone was no small factor. By themselves her comments were sharp, intelligent, in sync with the trendy values of the day. She had a knack for making cryptic quasi-academic asides. Asked by a Guardian journalist about branding and how it related to business operations, she had replied, "Capitalism is a perception. There is no underlying reality." What did it mean? No one knew, but they loved it! Except for Johanna, the business operations obsessive, who raged for days over the comment.

But Nicola's beauty, her *striking* beauty, sold more magazines than her comments, her reasoned approach to irrational emotional factors, her vivid idealism. Putting Nicola on the cover moved copies—her face transformed a stodgy business magazine into *Paris Vogue*. Balanced with her cool intellectual delivery, her command of numbers, her quotable phrases, her TED talks and her tweets, she dazzled. She seemed the idealized image of the visionary successful businesswoman. From the start, the press loved her.

Naomi Anan did not.

At least not at first. Michael was a homegrown entrepreneur, a natural, but he was well aware that trained educated entrepreneurs had an edge over even the most talented natural ones. He sent his staff to England to train and study at University, and one day he was challenged. If it made that much of a difference, why didn't he go himself?

He did. He took an MBA course in Scotland that required only a limited residency, but while there in person he had met Miss Naomi Watson. They met at Edinburgh while attending classes on pricing strategy. Michael had been totally absorbed in the lecturer. He was a business visionary, focused and evangelical, all books and studies. Nothing distracted him—but he distracted Naomi. Who *was* this man? He was like no one else. His accent, his gestures, his questions in class—he was radiant with individuality. And with something more— goodness. He had kind features, the kindest Naomi had ever seen. Each time he disappeared back to Ghana for weeks, a vacuum opened up inside Naomi. Would she never see him again? It took all of six months before she had the courage to approach him in the college library and suggest they study together.

They married two weeks later.

It was a happy marriage, and a secure one, made all the happier by Johanna, Benjamin and Jacob. Naomi had intended to make a career of teaching business at university rather than building it in the outside world, and had indeed gotten her teaching degree and secured a post. But only part-time. Drawn inevitably into helping Michael with his captaincy of Chococoa, and facing the work of raising three children, Naomi's days were more than full. Like Michael, she was a laborer.

But she was also a wife, and a possessive one. And though she was an attractive woman in her own right, Nicola was in a category all her own. After Michael's first meeting with Nicola, Michael had raved to Naomi over dinner about her brilliance and his luck. After several more meetings with Nicola stretching late into the night, and even more raving, Naomi began to wince at the sound of Nicola's name.

A meeting between the two was inevitable, and scheduled, and as Naomi walked into the Starbucks by Victoria Station in London, she expected her suspicions and fears to be fully confirmed.

Not at all. Naomi walked away dumbfounded, almost puzzled.

She wanted to find out what made Nicola tick, why she cared about chocolate workers in Ghana, what she wanted out of it all, what Nicola felt for Michael, what Nicola felt *period*. And Nicola didn't seem to feel much of anything. She approached Naomi's table, introduced herself, and sat down and immediately began reeling off a set of consumer behavior statistics and talking in a monotone about depth psychology and packaging symbolism.

Naomi kept trying to pull Nicola into a normal conversation. With no luck whatsoever. Did she have hobbies? No. A husband? No. A boyfriend? No. Was she gay? No. What was her favorite movie? She never went to movies. What sports team did she favor? She didn't follow sports. What magazines did she enjoy reading? *The Journal of the Experimental Analysis of Behavior.*

Nicola didn't seem to *mind* the personal questions. She just answered, usually in words of one syllable, and went on to abstract business topics. Naomi could not figure her out. Nicola talked brilliantly about how Chococoa could increase market share to some quantifiable number by inspiring compassion, but the compassion was something she *analyzed*; even her own compassion was something she analyzed rather than felt. She *demonstrated* compassion, true; her allegiance to Michael's goals were measurable and palpable. On camera and before interviewers she seemed to exhibit some degree of passion about what she was doing. But in private she was devoid of passion. Nicola was not devoid of obsession, however. When she talked about the motivations of chocolate-buying public, the psyche of the European market, of different class-driven strata of consumer behavior, her intensity of focus made Naomi think of a very little girl watching an ant farm with total fixation.

But whatever she felt, she *talked* brilliantly. Convincingly. Naomi left feeling that Nicola did indeed know exactly what she was doing when it came to getting people to buy Chococoa products. She also left convinced that there was no chance whatsoever of Nicola coming between Michael and Naomi. Michael *was* a man of passion, and Naomi had experienced that passion. He was no more likely to expend it on Nicola than on an abacus, even an abacus dressed in a sexy negligee. Nicola was one of a kind—impressive, but strangely abstract. Like Michael, Nicola seemed perfectly pure of heart. It was there that they resonated, But unlike Michael, Nicola sometimes barely seemed to have a heart. Not one that Naomi could see.

But if she could secure and grow the company, thought Naomi, she could lack heart, kidneys and liver. Did Naomi trust her? Yes. Did she understand what drove her? Not in the slightest. Nicola was a complete blank. But a smart competent complete blank that was wholly focused on securing a better future for herself, her husband, and her children. That was enough.

7

Kwaku washed his face. A supplier had been late, *again*, and had called to apologize, tearfully, profusely. Kwaku told him not to concern himself about it in the least, and then called another associate and instructed him to cut the man's throat.

The following call launched a small standing team of former military recruits whose leader had trained with the Israelis. Kwaku directed them to assault the late supplier's headquarters. They were to take over operations if personnel there were cooperative. Or kill them all and burn the facilities to the earth if they were not.

The dead man would shortly be cut into a few dozen pieces, and the most revolting pieces would be artfully packaged and sent to appropriate locations by Federal Express. The cut-out tongue would go to the Accra journalist most likely to be assigned to look into the incident—it might encourage his own tongue to practice a certain discretion. Eyeballs? Those would go to the police most likely to be assigned to look into it--perhaps it would inspire them to look elsewhere. His family would have to realize in no uncertain terms that revenge was not a wise option, but Kwaku did not want to appear insensitive. No doubt they had had a sentimental attachment. He rubbed his chin and thought about it. He'd send along the man's heart. He had to send *something*. What is art without the artist's signature?

The water in the exquisite Carrere marble basin swirled elegantly to the pipes below. He turned off the flow of the water from the solid gold fixtures, and looked out at *it* in the large gilded Parisian mirror. Not his face—*it*. He always thought of the thing that looked back at him from the mirror as *it*, not really as a face at all, much less *his* face. That had been lost, lost in a dream of pain, many years ago. *Ah, poor face*, thought Kwaku. *Where have you gone?* Would he meet it again in Heaven, he wondered? Or in some other, more curious, region?

Kwaku had been born among the poorest of the poor in one of the most lawless districts of a Ghana still reeling from decolonization and successive military coups. His mother had prostituted herself to keep her children from starving, and two of his six sisters had starved anyway. His first memory was hunger, his second was a failed theft of food to satisfy that hunger, a failure that had nearly gotten him kicked to death. Somehow he lived.

Somehow he grew.

The only people with money on those streets were dealers of drugs, and so, of course, when he was old enough to realize what money was, he went where the money was, running packages and making deliveries before he was ten. He was a handsome boy and a quick runner and in time the dealers were using him to run not only drugs but small cash transactions from one location to another. The biggest of the dealers, a man called the Boss, took him under his wing. The boy had potential. You could see his intelligence in his handsome young face. He was smart.

But also ambitious. Too ambitious. Kwaku dreamed of taking his brother and his sisters out of Ghana, to Britain, or maybe America. But how? How, he pleaded, evening after evening, to the gods.

The gods were kind. One day a last-minute leak informed the Boss that the Boss' rooms were to be hit by a rival gang. As his men armed, the Boss opened his safe and gave a package to Kwaku. He lied about the contents, and Kwaku saw in his face that the Boss was lying, but Kwaku gave no sign. The Boss gave Kwaku instructions to deliver it immediately to an associate at a restaurant on the other side of Accra.

Kwaku ran out into the streets and toward the restaurant. But... no, *no*, it was Kwaku's *one chance*, in his small thin hands was *Europe*, was *America*. He dove into an alley, opened the package, and inside there was money—all the money in the world! He took the money, stuck it in a discarded can, hid it in a hole in the alley wall out of which a rat slithered and covered the opening. He wrapped the now-empty package up again, all in bare moments, and, saying a prayer, he ran into the streets and sidewalks and ran and ran and when he had worked up enough courage he threw himself into the high-speed Accra traffic. A car struck him, smashing his ribs, fusing together two bones in his vertebrae. He woke days later in the hospital.

The Boss's men visited. The package? It must have flown into the traffic, said Kwaku, onto the streets. Maybe someone opened it. What was in it? Did the Boss include his address, asked Kwaku? Maybe a good person would return it.

The Boss' men looked at one another. They left.

Kwaku lay in bed, dreaming. Of French baguettes. American cowboys.

After a few days of recuperation, the Boss sent a car to pick him up and take him home to his mother and his little brother and sisters.

But once on the road it turned in a different direction.

Soon there were cocoa trees with long green leaves casting flickering layers of emerald light and shade across Kwaku's face as he looked out past the window.

He asked the driver where they were going.

The driver said nothing.

Eventually they stopped at a shack far out of earshot in an isolated clearing among cocoa trees not yet ready to be picked. The driver pulled Kwaku, still weak, out of the car by his arm.

The torture lasted for hours, and failed.

It was not strength of will that kept Kwaku from confessing—he soon confessed to everything, anything, but by then his lips were smashed and his teeth were so broken he could not be understood. The pain was so all-consuming, so total and unbelievable, that he lost all sense of speech, all sanity, all identity.

Yes, the Boss had thought, it probably was an accident. Or maybe the rival gang had had someone follow him and run him down. It was a shame that it had to happen to Kwaku—such a smart, handsome boy.

But anyone who failed to deliver a package of money from the Boss was a dead man—everyone knew that. That was simply how things were. Kwaku's death was sealed in the book of fate the moment the package had left his fingers. He would now die: die, and leave a *spectacularly* disfigured corpse to confirm to everyone that the Boss meant business.

The Boss bore him no ill will. He supposed that Kwaku was probably innocent. But how things were was simply how things were.

His rationale meant nothing to Kwaku. Nothing meant anything any longer. Kwaku's universe was now one vast exploding sun of pain: words were no longer a part of it.

The torturer, told to strive to memorable effects, had brought along a blowtorch and pliers and a variety of dental instruments. But despite the request for a higher level of artistry from the Boss, the torturer was bored and uninterested. He had had a difficult week. Gambling losses, a toothache, a girlfriend who whined and whined. Why did life have to be so difficult? He couldn't get his problems off his mind. It made his head hurt. He did not feel inspired to high art; he went dully through the motions. After all it was just another job.

He ran the blowtorch over the boy's hands and face a few times, then used the blowtorch to light a cigarette. Kwaku's screams and cries interrupted his line of thought, and irritated him further. Children and those high-pitched voices! To alleviate his boredom, he burned his initials and then a daisy shape and then tried to burn a likeness of a Smiley Face into the boy.

But his boredom was not alleviated. All that *screaming* coming out of one young mouth! The torturer knew he was expected to linger, but he wanted to finish quickly tonight, and go home and relax. His girlfriend might whine, but she was a fair enough cook, and later on tonight there was a new episode of *Downton Abbey*.

He noticed a machete in the corner of the shed, and a scythe, and thought he might try one or the other for a bit of variety. He put the blowtorch down on the ground, and frowned. Decisions, decisions. He picked up the machete and slashed the blade over Kwaku's face over and over as he hummed "We Are The Champions" by Queen, chopping the roasted face the way you would chop a salad. The screaming only got louder.

That damned endless screaming. The torturer swore. He'd had enough. So much blood had streamed down Kwaku's throat from the slashed ribbons hanging from the remainder of his face that the vein could not clearly be seen; he twisted the machete about and slashed the boy's throat anyway. Had the torturer missed it? What of it? The brat was a bloody mess, finished and done for.

The torturer removed the ropes binding Kwaku, so as to throw the boy's limp body to the ground and spread his legs for a better angle from which to hack away his genitals to bring back to the Boss. But first the fingers. After that he could toss the body in the back of the truck outside. As he began chopping off Kwaku's fingers with the machete so as to remove the fingerprints, he bent down absentmindedly to reach over and move the still-burning blowtorch, lest the boy's twitches should knock it over, and as he did so he wondered about whether he should have fish or rice for dinner that night while watching television. Why not both?

And at that moment, some deep primordial part of Kwaku's brain disconnected to the sea of pain grabbed the nearby blowtorch and ran the flaming point across the man's eyes.

The man screamed and howled.

The torturer greased his hair with a pomade that was highly flammable. The rest of his head caught fire almost at once. He ran outside and danced a strange dance and soon he fell dead at the base of a cocoa tree.

What was it, thought Kwaku, what *spirit* or *god* or *superhuman will* was it, that had moved Kwaku's hand. What *power from the other side* lifted Kwaku up and set him limping step by bleeding agonizing step away through the cocoa trees? He had returned to that moment so many times since that day; he would return to it again till the end of his life. During that forest flight, hours passed, centuries, entire universes were born and died. Pain? It was not mere 'pain.' He remembered it not as pain at all, but as something outside all human experience, holy and transcendent, leaving all body and mind behind. He drifted through the trees, the leaves, like the wind, like a ghost, till there was no pain, no sun or moon, no Kwaku, only the long holy blackness.

When he woke again, he found himself in the hut of some frightened impoverished Ghanaian family. They were frightened, but they were Christians. They could not let a lone mangled boy die in the fields. They hid him and tended his wounds and some became infected, and he screamed and hallucinated, as gods and demons came to him and revealed *their* inhuman faces too. They whispered to him, eating his humanity, and he shrieked as it was torn away. But the screaming passed, the infections passed. Months passed. He recovered.

As soon as he could walk, he returned to his own family, his mother and his brother and his sisters. The Boss had killed them all too. He didn't have Kwaku's body to demonstrate to everyone how fearsome the Boss was. He substituted theirs.

Next Kwaku went to the alley. The rats had not gotten into the can. The Boss had not found the money. Kwaku found it.

He returned to the family that had taken him in. They would be poor no longer. Even now he still visited them in their glorious Western home in Dansoman, and sent notes of congratulation when their children graduated from the European universities to which he had opened the doors. But that was now. Back then he lived with them for the next few years, waiting, planning, biding his time. Growing stronger. Ever stronger.

And when the time came, he purchased several guns, and found several young boys like himself, boys who were hungry and desperate and who knew how to use guns. The Boss was right: his mangled face, his rasping voice, his horrible scars, did strike terror into them. Kwaku's lips could only twist into a scar of a smile with difficulty now, but he smiled. Their terror was a good thing. All terror was a good thing.

No one mistook the tall thin monstrosity for the handsome boy that had run through the streets for the Boss not so many years ago. It wasn't only the horrifying features that were different now. The monstrosity *thought*. It *brooded*. It planned.

It took months, several months, of making, till the plan's final execution. But in the end, the Boss was in a chair in a shed surrounded by cocoa trees. And it took him many *many* days to die.

But all good things must come to an end, Kwaku reflected. And as the Boss, in the last moments of life, peered out past the needles in his remaining eye at Kwaku's face, he gurgled his final words to Kwaku through the blood dripping across his lipless mouth:

"You will always be a monster."

Kwaku dragged his hands, his *claws*, across the boss' dying, screaming face.

A monster. *A monster.*

The words filled his heart with unholy joy.

8

Six months into Nicola's investiture as Director of Marketing and Public Relations at Chococoa Ltd., her secretary rang through.

Nicola pressed the blinking button.

"The FFTC representatives have just arrived, Madame Director," said the voice of Nicola's secretary.

"Let them in, please."

Three well-dressed gentlemen and a woman in business attire entered Nicola's London office.

Greetings were exchanged.

Everyone sat down.

"I've read through the documents you've sent me," began Nicola, "and I am intrigued."

The tallest of the gentleman nodded. He was a Ghanaian, and according to their NGO web site, his name was Doctor Jerry Mensa-Manama.

She expected him to talk about the many virtuous undertakings of his non-profit organization, Freedom For The Children, but he said nothing, waiting for her to continue.

She did. "At Chococoa," she went on, "we believe that treating people well is not only worthwhile in itself, but is good for business. So we believe in supporting organizations and efforts that do good in the communities where our farmers and factories and projects are located."

"Putting an end to child trafficking is surely such a effort," said the second Ghanaian, nodding vigorously.

"Indeed it is," said Nicola, then got directly to the point. "That's... what intrigues me about your organization. Many organizations such as yours approach us with requests for financial support. But, unlike yourselves, they don't—how can I put it?—*guarantee* results."

Her visitors looked at one another. The first gentleman, the silent one, smiled broadly but still said nothing.

"We do," said the second Ghanaian.

"Yes," said the third Ghanaian.

"Would such results be of interest to you?" said the second Ghanaian.

Of course, thought Nicola. Child traffickers were not merely scum—they were a knife at the throat of Chococoa. Traffickers kidnapped children by the thousands off the street, or bought them from impoverished parents unable to support them. The traffickers sold them to farmers who used them as literal slave labor. It was everything Chococoa stood against and fought against.

But, reducing the numbers of enslaved children and the operations of their traffickers was also economically beneficial. It cost Chococoa a good deal to pay its workers. Competitors who used slave labor paid a good deal less, almost nothing, barely dispensing enough funds to keep the beaten and malnourished child slaves from starvation. Nonetheless, beans picked by a work force of slaves meant lower labor costs. The beans the children gathered could be sold for a fraction of what Chococoa charged. And so the buyers of cocoa beans bought them and looked the other way. The market goes where prices are low.

Nicola had given Chococoa a public relations boost by highlighting their supportive policies toward employees. The image and coverage translated into more sales, and governmental support. Nonetheless, the cheap labor and lower competitor pricing continued to gouge deeply, almost fatally, into the company's chances of survival. Whatever served to reduce child trafficking enhanced Chococoa's competitive edge, and increased its market share. Nicola had raised public awareness about the practice, and that helped. But any serious reduction ultimately lay in the hands of the politicians and the police of Ghana, some of whom were bribed by traffickers, others of whom were overwhelmed with other, equally pressing, problems.

Yet *these* people, FFTC, claimed to be able to make a difference. A *measurable* difference. Quickly.

"I'd like to know how you plan to achieve these worthy goals," said Nicola.

The three men smiled at one another. The woman did not smile.

"Suffice it to say: we have a large number of... activists, yes, at the ground level. They are more aware of the traffickers' activities than the authorities," said the second man.

"Much more aware," added the woman.

" –And can assist them in in breaking up such undertakings."

"Who exactly are these activists, and how many of them are active?"

The man spread his hands. "I regret to say that revealing their names would put them in jeopardy."

Nicola looked from one face to the other.

"I'm sorry," she said. "We do donate to activist groups, generously, but if you can't inform us of exactly what you do—"

Now the first man spoke up.

"You misunderstand, Madame Director. We do not want you to make donations to us. *We* want to make donations to *you*."

Nicola's head tilted, and her eyebrow rose.

"We have more than members and activists," he said. "We have donors. Many donors. No, not only people of wealth alone! We approach people on the street level every day and ask for contributions. The opposition to child trafficking is stronger and wider than you know. It is passionate! People sacrifice. We generate a good deal of street donation money, Madame Director."

"A good deal," added the second man.

"But," said the first, "because we are so 'grass-roots' an organization we do not have the..."—he searched for the right words—"the contacts, the prestige, of Chococoa. So. We would like to propose a partnership. We will supply the funds we gather to you; and you will direct them to firms and activities that support our efforts to save the children."

"We would be happy to allow you to take a certain percentage of those donations as a fee," said the second man. "Two percent? Five percent?"

"We *do* ask one thing, Madame Director. We wish to retain veto power over any given choice of recipient you may make. We would rather see funds for our children go to those groups and people who we feel can help our children."

"Yes," said the third man. He smiled. "We like Greenpeace too, you know? But the children come first. Yes?"

"And," said the second man, "also, while we would like you to assist in distributing a good deal of our funds, we will of course be keeping some donated funds we receive in our own hands, and using them to combat child trafficking locally."

Nicola sat back. Her inclination was to accept at once. What was the downside? Distributing money for a good cause was good, and would draw even more positive media attention to Chococoa and its worthy goals. It even gave Chococoa an additional income stream. Not a grand one, most likely, and she might well elect to waive the fee, purely out of good will—and to further advance Chococoa's charitable image.

"Of course there will have to be some discussion with the board, gentleman, Madame, but—"

Nicola stopped and shook her head. No, their offer fit her criteria perfectly. It was very good for Chococoa. It was very good for others. No, only a fool would hesitate.

"Do you have a formal proposal ready, gentlemen? Miss?"

The woman opened a briefcase and took out a sheaf of papers.

9

Freedom For The Children delivered. The results of their partnership with Chococoa were so fast and so impactful they were almost shocking. Whatever sort of grass roots fundraising these people were doing, it bordered on genius. Six-figure packages began arriving like clockwork. Not that the impact of their profit margins was particularly great. It was not a part of Chococoa's principal operations, and Nicola gave it only a part of her attention. She left the general oversight and distribution of funds to a promising newly hired young man called Chris in Financial. The Freedom people seemed very happy with him—partly, thought Nicola, because so far he'd taken their list of recommended beneficiaries at face value and dispersed the funds readily.

Nicola was not entirely pleased. Chris was a

wizard in some respects, but he was like a switchblade: lightning-fast, but so fast you could cut your fingers. He had a brilliant talent for finding data that supported the initiatives Nicola wanted to undertake, and burying the data that did not support them somehow in the shadows without ever quite erasing it. It was an ambiguous skill, but useful, and she considered him an ally. But he had weaknesses. As far as Freedom For The Children went, he seemed to do very little research on the recipients of the funds; she needed to talk to him about that.

But that was a mere process technicality. What was truly astounding was the impact on the child traffickers—assuming there was a direct impact, that it was not mere coincidence. Whatever the cause, things seemed to go exactly as the spokesman for Freedom For The Children had promised. Reports of exposures and arrests involving child trafficking networks began to dot the Ghanaian newspapers. Competitors relying on trafficker-enabled labor for their supply chains found them constantly, radically, disrupted.

Nicola was not entirely comfortable with the details of those breakups. There seemed to have been a spate of assassinations of leading traffickers. Some farmers using child labor were found murdered. Nicola was concerned that the anti-trafficking efforts of Freedom For The Children might unintentionally be inspiring vigilante action.

But the carnage was too systematic for vigilantes. Apparently some sort of gang war was going on between the traffickers. They seemed to literally be shooting one another down in the streets.

Chococoa had nothing to do with it, however; and if any tips from the streets that Freedom For The Children had garnered had had an impact, it could not be quantified. What mattered to Chococoa from a commercial standpoint was that their competition was in chaos. Their disarray was only positive. Some of the biggest firms in the world chocolate industry had depended, knowingly or not, in small part or large, on child slave labor. Now that labor force was being seriously disrupted, and Nicola's campaigns pointed out their competitors' malfeasance and Chococoa's moral leadership and virtue. It raised Chococoa even higher in the public estimation—and sold more product.

They were making money. And transforming Ghana for the better.

For a rare and unexpected moment, Nicola examined her feelings.

And that was the shocking thing.

She was happy.

10

Jacob yawned. It was nearly three in the morning. He'd been listening to Johanna wax eloquent about supply chains and simulation modeling for hours.

"C'mon, Jo, let's hit the cots. This supply chain stuff is not that hard," he said.

"Oh, really," said Johanna, her voice dripping with sarcasm.

Jacob smiled. To her surprise, he said, "It's because I have such a good teacher."

Johanna looked up from the screen. She didn't know what to say.

"No, really. This simulation modeling is pretty cool," he said. "I do see how it all works now. At least I see it better. How everything hangs together."

"Then let's go through it one more time," said Johanna. Her finger traced a line along the flowchart on the screen.

"The farmers plant the seeds and grow the trees on their land," she said. "They hire people to harvest the cocoa pods. The workers open the pods and take the cocoa beans out and put them on the ground. They put the trees' leaves over them and let them dry. Then they put the dried beans in bags and send them to the warehouse. The warehouse sifts through the beans to kick out any bad or diseased ones. Then they put the beans in fresh bags and ship them to our factory at Derby where they turn the cocoa beans to milk chocolate and dark chocolate and so on. That's not the whole process, or every little detail of the process. But that's how it works. And how we can examine it and think about how to improve it."

"Got it," said Jacob.

"Good. So tell me, Jacob. How *would* you improve this process? What could you do to improve quality and efficiency? To reduce costs?"

Jacob crossed his arms. "Buy the land ourselves? Not use farmers. Cut out the middleman."

"Land's expensive. Government officials get involved. And who'll run the farm? We don't have the farmers' expertise."

"We could buy land from retiring farmers. Keep them on as consultants. We'd get our feet wet, learn the ropes, and gradually we'd own more and more land directly."

"Not bad! You're thinking in the long-term, though. What can we do for an *immediate* improvement?"

"Hm. Plastic film over the cocoa beans, instead of leaves? If it lets sunlight in, the beans could dry faster and they move along the chain faster."

"*Very* good." She made a note. "We'd have to factor in the cost of the plastic, and find a vendor, and experiment to see the optimal time for drying, and whether the sun might have negative effects, like burning some percentage of the beans. Anything else?"

"Develop pods with more beans?"

"You're talking either plant breeding, which can be very long term as well, or genetic modification—which has mixed market response, and can involve regulatory issues."

Jacob frowned. He yawned again. "I need to sleep on it. C'mon, Jo. You do too."

"I'll sleep when I'm buried."

Jacob grunted. "That may not be too long from now if we take a motorcycle back to the airport. What was *that* all about, Jo? That guy *hit* you. It wasn't an accident."

"Save the paranoia for spy movies, Mr. Mind Reader. Maybe the rider's just an idiot. Nobody kills people to keep them from inspecting cocoa beans."

"Maybe some do."

"What, you think Nicola put a hit contract out on us?"

Jacob laughed. "No, that's ridiculous. I don't know, could be anything. Maybe the driver just got fired, and when he saw your business suitcase on the bike rack he decided to strike a blow against The Capitalist Pig."

Johanna shrugged. "Who knows? Or cares. We're here to do a job."

"Speaking of which—."

"Yes?"

"I'm no supply chain expert, Jo…"

"Oh, after a few hours with Johanna Anan, by now you're a *full MBA*, Mr. Entrepreneur."

"But you've walked me through the supply chain that Chococoa is using, and—"

"And?"

"Well—it seems pretty tight. I mean, no offense, but I don't see a lot of ways to improve things. At least not immediately. Looks to me like Nicola's done a pretty sweet job."

Johanna frowned. Jacob was giving Nicola too much credit.

But she had to be honest with herself. Nicola did deserve *some*. It was Johanna who had done a sweet job a few years ago, analyzing and driving actual operations the way she was attempting to do now. Nicola had not really *interfered*, other than to continually cut funding or turn down Johanna's proposals. Johanna had assumed that once she left, Nicola would find herself out of her depth and the company would decline. And that had happened. But the decline was mysterious. Johanna's sound practices hadn't been discontinued, or radical changes made. There were *subtle* interferences from management, small, quiet changes that frustrated competent functioning.

Johanna shook her head. "I just don't get it," she said to Jacob. "Chococoa is—it's like a car whose oil never gets changed on time, or whose tires are shot and whose aging battery needs to be replaced. No individual problem is fatal, or even particularly noticeable. But collectively it's a spreading corrosion. If you understand the supply chain, you can *see* it. Like the trucks here. It's costing Chococoa more to repair them than to replace them with newer models. Or the light bulbs in the warehouse. You saw them flickering. What's the problem with just replacing them?"

"Maybe the operation here is broke."

"The operation here has enough money to send a helicopter to pick us up without blinking," said Johanna. "Besides, I have the budget here. There's enough for full-page ads in the *Accra Daily Mail* and the *Ghanaian Times*, but not for light bulbs? Nicola's not *that* dumb. It's like she's deliberately trying to make the company fall apart."

"Come on, don't be silly. She's even more of a nutcase workaholic than you are. Why sink your own company and put yourself out of a job?"

"The problem is, all these *little* problems can be fixed. That's what supply chain analysis points out: all those things that can be done better. It's all about *kaizen*, really—it's all about building up habits that foster continual small improvements. And what's been happening is that the details of our operations are being almost *systematically* neglected."

"The devil is in the details," said Jacob.

"The devil is in the *chain*," said Johanna. "You need to see the supply chain as a whole, Jacob. That's why I'm doing a simulation model. And what it's telling me is that there are a hundred *small* things that can be done to improve operations, a hundred easy changes that could make the difference that could save the company."

"Well, that's great!"

"Except I can't turn *all* of them around in a month. And I can't figure out how or why Nicola could let *hundreds* of these tiny inefficiencies creep into the chain in the first place."

Jacob leaned back and stretched. "You've just got Nicola on the brain. You always have. Lighten up. Maybe things have gone to pot just because they've gone to pot, like the way your room gets filled with junk, or the way your toes get grungy. Stop blaming Nicola for everything."

It was true. *Nicola* was the devil in the chain, as far as Johanna was concerned. When Johanna had been with the company she and Nicola had continually bumped heads and gotten into heated scraps. Every boardroom meeting was a pitched battle.

What *was* it about Nicola that set Johanna's teeth on edge so? Partly it was her beauty. Well, not her beauty so much as the way the press, Benjamin, Jacob, even her father, simply *swooned* over her and defended her. Partly it was her coldness. There was just something wrong there. Nicola had no life outside her jobs, her charts, her books and papers. She was opaque. Women couldn't see into her, and men didn't look any farther than the surface.

But Nicola wasn't *irrational*. If you could make a good case for a practice, she'd listen, and (more likely than not) adopt it. She was not incompetent. She hadn't been incompetent in the beginning, anyway.

The supply chain she and Jacob had examined hadn't fallen from outer space. Michael had set up the foundation, and it was a sound foundation. Johanna had been adding her input ever since she opened her first book on supply chain management, and her input had seeped in: the way they operated *still* owed a good deal to Johanna. It had been set up well. Not perfectly, not as well as she could set it up now, but adequately.

But *was* Nicola the devil in the chain? Three years ago Johanna blew up and left, and she had expected, had *hoped,* that Nicola would interfere and wreck everything and that Johanna would be called back in weeks. But weeks had passed, then months, and that proved not to be the case.

Nicola had done something that Johanna had not expected her to do—she had done nothing.

So things went on as before, slowly, quietly, corroding. Yes, some processes had decayed, and others had gotten buggy, and reporting clearly needing updating. But a well set-up supply chain tends to persist. Nothing was *deeply* wrong.

Why the rise in costs then? Because of things outside of their control. The price of global chocolate futures had gone haywire, plunging almost 40%. Oil prices, and therefore transport prices, had risen. Nicola hadn't upgraded the technology—any of it. That saved money initially, and the first year after Johanna left things actually looked better. But trucks and sorting machines were having more expensive breakdowns more often now. Outdated computers were failing to run updated programs.

It all *hurt.* And the hurt was puzzlingly consistent, and across the board. But even so all of it together didn't add up to bankruptcy.

She sighed. Maybe tomorrow would tell a different story. She and Jacob were going into the fields. If there was one thing Johanna knew about simulation modeling it was that the model didn't always perfectly reflect the underlying reality of the process. The numbers might say one thing. Eyeballing the chain directly would tell you something else. Always. Not always what you were looking for, not always something important and life-saving, but always something.

At least she *hoped* that that would happen, that it was something simple and easy to spot. Time was of the essence. The clock was ticking. The closer they approached the deadline, the easier it would be to miss the key element needed. And to lose everything.

If there was a key element. And not this strange collection of minor inefficiencies. She had envisioned the problem as a lion that she could take down with a single shot. But increasingly it seemed as though the problem was a horde of Army Ants. She could stop one, she could stop dozens, but she couldn't stop all of them overnight. The only solution there was time, and it was running out,

Her eyes roved over the screen yet again, and she pressed a key, transitioning from slide to slide, trying to find something. Something anomalous. Something *major.*

But there were only two real anomalies that Johanna could spot. And neither was critical. She couldn't explain them. But then who could explain what went on inside Nicola's crazy head anyway?

Maybe another idiot.

"Hey, Sleepyhead," said Johanna.

"Umm?" said Jacob, who had dozed off in his chair.

"Tell me, Mr. Supply Chain Expert, I've taken you through the process. Have you noticed anything odd? Anything you can't account for?"

"Well—yeah, I guess."

"Enlighten me."

"Expenditures. I can understand spending on jute bags and worker housing and stuff like that. But what is *this?* 'Freedom For The Children'?"

"I remember that name from somewhere. Sounds like one of those crazy charities Nicola is always giving talks to and spending the company PR money on. *PR,*" growled Johanna. Her lip curled.

"Didn't I hear something once about them supposedly giving money to *us* for something or other? The numbers here say she's directed over $100,000 of local company funds to them so far just this year."

"She says it's for PR. That Chris can show that there's

a direct correlation between money to them and profit margin for us."

"She can say what she wants, dude, but that's six figures. Six figures is a lot to spend on charity when you're going under."

"Six figures won't keep us from going under one way or another, but you're right that that level of spending right now makes no sense."

"It's offset a little by some income that's actually coming into us *from* that source, though. See there?"

"But that's strange too. Businesses donate to charity. What kind of charity donates *to* businesses?

"Should I see if they have an office in Accra? We could stop by and have a look."

Johanna pursed her lips. "Yes. Do it. When you wake up. Notice anything else?

"Shipping. Our trucks are carrying additional stuff for some other company. What for? Why don't we just go straight to ship?"

"Apparently we're in a partnership. That *could* make economic sense, I guess. Sharing the cost of delivery. Except I don't see where they pay anything in, or how we make any cost savings over before."

"Are we giving them a free ride?"

"*That* doesn't make economic sense at *all*. But we can look into that some more when we get to that step in the chain."

"Great," said Jacob, stretching. "So we can finally black out."

He stood up and stretched. "Good *night*, Johanna!"

She grunted, and pulled up an Excel chart. She stared at the numbers. It wasn't anything major. It wasn't even major enough to be minor.

But Jacob was right. It didn't make any economic sense.

Was it simple oversight?

"Hey Jo—"

"Shut up and go to sleep."

"What if that cyclist that rammed you *is* a hit man? Nicola really *is* trying to kill us? Would that be, like James Bond cool or *what?*"

"It would certainly eliminate one expensive and unnecessary element of the supply chain."

"What?"

"Your big mouth."

Chapter Four

The Meeting

1

"Nicola?"

"Not now, Chris," said Nicola. "I have to get ready for my flight."

It was to be Nicola's first-ever visit to Ghana, and it would cap her triumph. Everything was going well. Beyond well. Chococoa sales were up, Chococoa stores were expanding in number, Chococoa was getting Likes on Facebook and trending on Google. Fan pages on Tumblr were appearing. Almost every day there was a dazzling photograph of Nicola in prominent business publications. Chococoa was becoming part of the mental environment, like Coke, like Pepsi.

And best of all—Johanna, that ever-nagging thorn in her side, was finally *gone*, resigning last week in a fit of uncontrolled babyish fury. Nicola now led the company.

And she had every intention of making it the company Michael Anan had wished: ethical, fair, superlative in quality.

It was intoxicating—thrilling.

"But, I mean, like… it's, like, something you kind of

should *know*—?"

Chris looked up at her with those sad chipmunk eyes, that absurd trembling lower lip.

"Oh all right, Chris. What is it?"

"Well, it's about those spreadsheets you asked for. About Freedom For The Children? I have them here."

"It certainly took them enough time to forward them."

"Uh huh. Well, there are... oddities."

Nicola looked away from the paperwork she was putting into her briefcase, the material she would be working on during the plane flight, and snatched the folio Chris was holding and thumbed through the spreadsheets briefly. She straightened, and her head tilted.

"Chris, these amounts come to *millions*."

"That's what we're receiving in our accounts, and that's what we're distributing. There's more coming too. All the time. We're... uh... projecting that it's going to hit tens of millions, at this rate. Annually."

"That's more profit than all Chococoa generates."

"Yes, Ma'am."

"Where are they getting all this money?"

"I don't know, Ma'am."

"Have you asked?"

"Well... not really. My directions—um, from *you*— were only to redistribute it to listed charitable groups. With the advice and consent of the FFTC people, of course. I mean, I've sort of asked, like, *casually*. But they haven't been, like, forthcoming."

Nicola always thought in terms of perception first. *Chococoa is distributing millions to charity. Therefore millions now see Chococoa in terms of charity, compassion, humanity.*

Well, what was wrong with that? A smile nearly broke across her perfect features. Her tiny decision had turned into a triumph of branding. A spectacular one. No wonder sales of Chococoa were skyrocketing.

But still... passersby on the street in Ghana couldn't

be donating *that* much. Had some private Ghanaian billionaire left them a bequest? Had they done a merger? She couldn't do business with them if they were no longer primarily a charity. Ethics were ethics.

"I'll talk to the FFTC people when I arrive at Ghana. Set up an appointment for me, will you, Chris?"

"Yes, Ma'am."

Nicola's debut in Ghana was spectacular— everything she dreamed and more. The press met her plane in droves as it landed in Accra. Her pictures appeared on the front-page in all the papers. She toured the farms and the fields in a pith helmet and short pants showing off her long exquisite legs, like Grace Kelly in an American Hemingway movie from the Fifties. She spoke with few actual workers, true, but then everywhere she went, young boys and girls ran up to her with flowers, forming a smiling cocoon, sometimes breaking into songs of welcome. Mornings were spent talking to Chococoa managerial staff, afternoons were like catwalk photo-shoots by Ghanaian landmarks. In the evenings she would give passionate speeches about how ethical business practices could lift up the Ghanaian people to ground-breaking new heights, and how Chococoa was the model showing the way. The visit was turning into an absolute triumph.

So much so that she completely overlooked the scheduled meeting with the Freedom For The Children group. It was with a surprise that she heard an assistant inform her that the scheduled meeting was now a half hour away. Should she skip it for another round with the press, another set of photographs by a historic site?

It was tempting. Ghana *delighted* her. There was so much to see, so much to say.

But she would not be Nicola if she did not keep to schedule. Managing a company, like managing perceptions, was nothing if not a systematic undertaking. Nothing if not a hands-on task. She had come to Ghana not to be delighted but to generate wide and positive attention for Chococoa—and, she privately reflected, to strengthen the public's perception that Nicola and Chococoa were one. That would stabilize her dominance. Help her lead. Give the company a face, the way Steve Jobs was the face of Apple. It was not vanity on her part. The public mind responded to faces. It would help Chococoa. Help Michael. Help Ghanaians.

A kind of joy, so rare, coursed through her. She had succeeded. Magnificently. But Johanna's shadow continued to tug at her elbow. Practicalities, less glamorous company functions, mattered as well; and managing cash flow properly was not the least of them. A talk with Freedom For The Children would be appropriate due diligence; and would let people see that Nicola was taking care of that aspect of her role too.

Yes, she could spare twenty minutes. "Arrange for a vehicle."

Nicola had imagined some small corporate office, but the limousine pulled up in front of one of the tallest buildings in all Ghana. She had also imagined that the Freedom For The People organization would have had people waiting outside, beaming, to greet her. That the usual host of press and photographers and cameramen would be streaming the whole visit live. Some of the passersby outside did notice her from all the recent pictures in the papers, but most were indifferent. There was not even a small entourage to greet her.

It didn't matter. Business was business. She took the folio Chris had prepared and stepped up a few steps up and passed across the entrance into the building.

Again, no one greeted her, although several eyes followed her as she walked to the elevators. She dismissed them as the usual looks that testosterone-driven men and envious women cast her way. Security seemed unusually high, with armed guards of an almost military bearing. Odd. To guard a charity? But then perhaps there were other residents more in need of such security. In any event no one stopped her as she located Freedom For The Children on a vast plaque listing the building's companies and residents.

She pressed the button. The elevator doors opened. She entered.

The security men stared at her as they closed.

Several moments passed. The doors opened.

Nicola stepped out into a large empty hallway.

It was elegant and modern and meticulously clean.

No one was there.

She walked past a series of abandoned offices in silence. They seem to have been recently occupied: there were cups of coffee on the desks, scattered folders and paperwork. Freedom For The Children was stamped across various marketing collateral in multiple languages. Windows and Macintosh logos revolved on the screens of state-of-the-art computers. Phone consoles blinked. Air conditioners hummed.

"Hello?" she called.

It was as though everyone had vanished.

"Is anyone here?"

No answer.

She checked the appointment scheduler on her smartphone. Had she gotten the location right? Yes. She was on time as well. The meeting was to be held at a Room 101 on the facilities. She looked at the numbers on the nearest doors and headed in the direction they suggested. Nicola passed a large expanse of cubicles, all full of active equipment, all completely devoid of people, and at the end turned to her right. There was Room 101.

She hesitated. She felt a coldness. Why? She suddenly remembered that Room 101 was the room in George Orwell's *1984* where Winston Smith was tortured, his head shoved into a box full of rats. She smiled at her apprehension. Assuming this *was* the right place, and even assuming the talk turned out poorly, the meeting was not likely to turn out quite *that* poorly.

Silly, she thought. She reached out for the doorknob and turned it and half-opened the door.

From behind her a large dark hand dropped on her shoulder.

Her heart jumped to her throat, and she nearly screamed.

Her head swiveled and she saw the rest of the man and again a scream rose, half-strangled in her throat. The man seemed six and a half feet tall, and nearly as wide, and towered over Nicola.

He had the frame of a bodybuilder, and while the business suit draped over it was expensive and immaculate, it seemed as though all he had to do was take a deep breath for the massive muscles to tear through the material. His head was bullet-shaped and shaven, his nose broken, his eyes were dead and merciless.

In his other hand was a something that looked like a toy pistol in that tremendous palm.

It was a sawed-off shotgun with a pistol butt instead of a stock.

She opened her mouth. He shoved her through the door and she went sprawling to the floor.

He closed the door behind them.

The room trembled. Nicola looked around. It was not a room at all, but a box. And with a jerk, the box *moved*. A moment's disorientation, and she realized that Room 101 was not a room at all, but an elevator, lifting.

Nicola half-rose. There was a tear in her stocking. The *imperfection* of it, the damage to her look, struck her like a slap. The feeling was a Band-Aid, blotting out her confusion, her fear, her rising terror. She did not want to look past it, to the man with the shotgun, standing there breathing heavily.

The elevator stopped and one of its walls opened. She sprawled into it, away from the huge silent man. The room was subtly lit, almost dark, a boardroom like the one at Chococoa, with a long gleaming table and a dozen elegant corporate chairs along the side. At the far end of the conference table, a figure was sitting. A dark blur.

She stared.

Quietly a recessed lamp opened an aureole of light on the person at the far end of the table, and the light grew stronger and stronger. Nicola continued to stare, her heart beating, transfixed. It was a man, a man holding a cup of tea. The light grew stronger. She began to make out his face—

Now she did scream.

She scrambled to her feet and turned and ran. The man with the shotgun grabbed her with his free hand and threw her again to the floor, hard. Her shoulders shivered. She felt the onset of a panic attack.

"*Nicola,* my dear," said the voice at the end of the table. It was rich, resonant, almost Shakespearean. "Come, come," it murmured, with exaggerated kindness. "Such a fuss. You came to ask some questions, did you not? Here they all are, waiting to be revealed, and you snivel there like a child."

She stiffened and rose. *My God—*that *face.*

"I—I don't know who you think you are—"

"I know exactly who I am," said the rich deep voice. "I am your owner. Your master. I am the organ grinder and you are my monkey."

"What—"

There was an explosion in the back of her head. It slammed her forward onto the conference table. She tried to raise a shaking hand to the patches of throbbing pain at the back of her head, but her hands seemed out of her control.

"Thank you, Jerry," said the man. "Jerry, my associate, has just shot two shotgun blasts into the back of your head, Nicola. Not *quite* blanks—I had him stuff them with paper pellets instead of steel ones. Otherwise you wouldn't have a head now. The paper pellets are just enough to disorient without causing lasting damage or disfiguration. After all, we don't want to mar that *lovely* hair of yours. Or the head underneath it. Not yet. Not while it remains of service. Hear that sound?"

Nicola could hear metallic rasping, and then a sharp *click*.

"*Those* shells are filled with broken glass. Jerry?"

The large man grabbed Nicola by the hair, slammed her on the conference table, and put the barrels of the shotgun against her face. Nicola screamed.

"Do we understand our relative positions now, Nicola, dearest?"

"*Yes. Yes!*" she shrieked.

The man at the far end snapped his fingers. His associate flicked Nicola away like a used cigarette.

"I am Kwaku," said the man at the far end of the table.

He interlaced his fingers, placed his chin on his hands, and tilted his head rather elegantly.

"I can end your life at any moment with a single word. With a snap of my fingers."

He raised a hand and placed his thumb and middle finger together.

"Want to see?"

Nicola cringed.

"But why take life when you can fill it with pain and horror instead? Understand this, Nicola, darling: I can make the manner of your death as painful as the human mind can imagine. I can make that pain last for weeks, for months, for the rest of your life. I can tear off your arms and legs, tear out your eyes and tongue. I can make your face look like *my* face, Nicola. No matter where you are, no matter where you hide, I can eradicate you from the face of the earth. You exist only because I allow you to exist, and you will continue to exist for exactly as long as I wish it. And so, from this moment on, you will do *exactly* what I *order* you to do. Do you understand?"

Her head was reeling, her eyes began to tear; vomit rose in her throat.

She uttered a gargled sound.

"Do you understand?"

"Y-yes. Yes."

"Excellent," said the man. "Jerry? Could you freshen my Earl Grey, please?"

The massive figure went to a tea service behind the man with the scarred face, put down his shotgun, poured tea and delivered it to Kwaku, then took the used cup back to the service and resumed his previous position.

Kwaku sipped, and smacked his lips. "Ah!"

He resumed. "Nicola—my dear—the organization you wished to visit is a facade. Not entirely a facade. I've dressed it up with enough resources to pass a casual inspection. But its real purpose is not its ostensible one. Its real purpose is to take the money that my endeavors have raised through a variety of extralegal means, and pass them through channels allowing me to re-distribute them legally and globally."

"You're laundering funds," whispered Nicola. "Criminal funds."

"Yes. Oh, *some* small part of the money the organization here supposedly raises does in fact come from street donations and the like, but the vast, vast bulk are payments for illicit drugs, fees for paid executions, sexual services—whatnot. One can't really take such funds to the Bank of England. Bankers report to governments and governments ask all sorts of impolite questions about where so much currency all came from. Thanks to this little charity of ours, we can say that we raised the funds by thousands and thousands of freely given small donations, and through occasional large gifts from anonymous donors. And the powers that be believe us. They believe us because the people receiving the funds and directing them to various recipients and charitable groups—other facades that we operate—is the celebrated Chococoa, a world-renowned corporation known for its ethics, its charity, its humanism. What could be more above board?"

Nicola felt cold, a cold that passed through her limbs

like ice water.

"The charity. It's all a lie," she said in a flat voice.

"Oh, not at *all*," said Kwaku. His lips twisted in some horrible configuration Nicola realized was what passed for a smile. "Not at *all*. Every *good* facade *needs* some relation to reality. As I said, some funds do come our way through donations. Why, every time you make one of your dazzling speeches some buffoon of a society matron or trendy activist writes us a fat check. Freedom For The Children *does* free some children, and feeds some others, and operates a number of schools, and provides a variety of scholarships. Those facades are not its main purpose, however. Merely an operating expense."

Dark anger welled in Nicola's throat.

"Do you traffic in *children* as *well*, you *bastard!*" she shouted.

Kwaku looked at the man with the shotgun. "Jerry? If you please?"

The man grabbed Nicola by her stylish collar, slammed her against the wall, and threw a punch that slammed into her belly like a log flying out of a chute. Nicola gasped, choked, and fell to her knees and vomited.

The man put down his shotgun, removed a handkerchief from his pocket, and gently wiped her lips. He picked her up and sat her in a Naugahyde chair near Kwaku, and picked up his shotgun again.

"He's really quite expert, you know," said Kwaku. "You won't have any visible bruises. Or even a ruptured spleen. Unless I request it, of course. One word, and you'll have to have to wear a colostomy bag for the rest of your life. But to answer your question, my darling— no, I don't traffic in children. I had rather a difficult childhood here myself," he said, pointing to his face, "as you may imagine."

Nicola tried to speak, but could only cough.

"I like children," continued Kwaku. "In fact, reducing child trafficking in Ghana was something I had long been inclined to do," continued Kwaku. "But of course one prefers to do things that are cost-effective. The fiscal aspect of it *nagged* at me, and then one day I became aware of your company. Your struggling fatuous pricey little firm. It would never have survived in its market struggles against your competitors in the chocolate industry here. Their child slavery practices simply made their labor costs too cheap compared to yours.

"But, I reflected, if I could *help* your firm survive," said Kwaku, "and it agreed to accept and transfer some of my funds, then I could launder assets to my heart's content, *and* incidentally exterminate some vermin I would rather enjoy exterminating. And agree you did. So I killed leading traffickers left and right, and made it look like they were killing each other in gang wars. Soon they *were* killing each other in gang wars, generously lowering my ammunition costs. Child trafficking fell into complete chaos, your competitors' cheap labor supply collapsed, their operations faltered— voilà: Chococoa, untouched, rose to splendid ethical heights and stellar profits. And Kwaku laundered many many millions of euros."

A look of tragic understanding crossed Nicola's pale features.

"Oh—you thought it was *you* that built up the firm? No, dear. It was Kwaku."

Nicola coughed up a drop of blood trying to say something. She failed.

Kwaku turned his scarred and blackened Autumn leaf of an ear her way.

"What was that you said? Thank you? Oh, you're entirely welcome, my dear!"

He clapped his hands together.

"Now, however, I wish to take things to a higher level. And do you know what you can do to assist, Darling?"

She shook her head.

"Nothing!" he said. "Nothing at all. You simply need to keep your attractive little nose *out* of my dealings with Chococoa. Otherwise I will tear it off. And to ensure that you have truly learned that lesson, your passive involvement in Freedom For The Children will now become a more active one. A percentage of Chococoa's profits will now regularly be donated to our operation. Exactly how much? Hm. I haven't decided yet. But a *generous* amount. After all, we've given so much to you. It's time to give back."

Nicola was still unable to speak. But she could move her head. She let it fall, and pressed her lips together and shook her head from right to left, left to right. No.

No.

Kwaku sighed.

"Jerry?"

The huge figure of his subordinate turned and placed his shotgun on the floor again and reached under the table and brought out a can of gasoline. He placed it on the table. Then he grabbed Nicola by the collar and dragged her up and lay her on her back on the table in front of Kwaku.

She struggled, but a hard slap across her face reduced her to a pathetic bleating of whimpers.

Kwaku sipped his Earl Grey.

"You know, Nicola," he said, "I'm your greatest fan. Really, I am. I've read your articles. Your papers. I follow your speeches. That TED talk you gave! Wonderful. 'Appearance and reality.' What profound subjects. You know, I've always felt that you—with your perfect loveliness—and I, with this mass of scar tissue I call a face, have a certain kinship. A symmetry. Our looks make us what we are, don't you think? They've defined us. Shaped our path. Our destinies. Beauty and the Beast!"

He took a box of matches from his pocket and nodded to Jerry. Jerry splashed gasoline over Nicola's face. She choked and twisted and Jerry held her down.

Kwaku struck a match.

He slowly lowered it to a quarter of an inch from her face.

She screamed like some insane creature.

"Beautiful, beautiful Nicola. So pretty," whispered Kwaku. "Now you will look just like me."

"*No!*" she screamed.

"No?"

"*I'll do anything you want!*" shrieked Nicola, tears streaking her face, foam across her lips. "*Anything!*"

Kwaku held the match there for a moment. He pitied her. He pitied her so much he nearly let go of the match. All he had to do was let go, and she would be free. Free of her beauty, free of the companionship of others, free of affection and love and community, free of the things of this world. Free of humanity—of her own humanity. Free like Kwaku.

But that would not be a wise business decision.

He sighed, and blew out the flame.

"Jerry, please take our visitor somewhere where she can clean up, and then show her out."

He looked at Nicola and again made that smear of twisted flesh that passed for his smile.

"We will speak again."

2

Nicola was gone. Kwaku sat back in his resplendent Naugahyde throne alone. He sipped his tea. He looked down at the conference table in thought. He could see his reflection in the polished tabletop, like a ghost captured in onyx.

What have I become? he thought. So many times, looking at his shattered remains of his face in the mirror, or in the aftermath of sessions much, much more horrible than this one with Nicola, he would think, happily: *I have become a monster.* It was a happy thought because once one ceases to be a man, one has no alternative other than becoming a god. *Are not the gods monsters too?*

But more and more, he found an additional answer to that question, a new role to play: he thought, *I am a king.*

A brutal, Shakespearean king emerging from a brutal Ghanaian underworld. But emerging into what? Yes, his drug operations had been the origins of a fortune, but as the money grew the operations expanded outside those operations into above ground business entities. He used Chococoa to launder funds. Nicola might have left well enough alone, but women are curious, like cats. Eventually, he supposed, he would have to take it over entirely, seed it with his people, dispense with its existing leadership. The parasite over time becomes the host. Just as the criminal who bribes the police and government long enough *becomes* the police and the government.

Kwaku could truthfully say that, apart from the Boss who had torn away his face and tossed it to the gods, he bore no ill will toward the people he had gone on to torture, blackmail, or execute. He terrorized people, yes, but only so as to gain their compliance and secure their cooperation. The victims regarded the tiger's teeth as cruel, but he, Kwaku, the tiger, did not. This was how he survived in the territory he had marked as his own. It was how things were.

But the larger his operations grew, the less the need for terror and the more for simple competent management. He created the facade of Freedom For The Children not only to launder funds; he remembered with bitterness his own unfreedom as a child—and yes, he *did* enjoy exterminating the more vicious of the traffickers.

But now he found himself running an organization that *did* save children, and fed and educated them, and generated *actual* donations. He had bribed government officials to look the other way at his operations.

Newly elected ones needed no persuading. They supported his good works actively! Between the bribery and the good will, he was penetrating into the viscera of Ghana's political bureaucracy more and more. Soon the day would come when he could direct the government itself in whatever direction he wanted.

Should he? What *was* that direction?

What *did* he want?

He really had studied Nicola and her methods. Studied them meticulously. A brilliant woman. He was pleased he had not had to kill her, or maim her as he had been maimed. Paper pellets in a shotgun, ominous lighting, a deep voice trained by a drama coach, a splash of gasoline, a match. Yes, there had been that blow to the stomach, but she had been *rude*. For the most part it was all show. Play the part of the sinister villain, and the rest of the players will play along. All of Ghana that knew of Kwaku *feared* Kwaku, and all because of these petty dramatics. When it was his *mind* that they needed to fear, and the directions in which he chose to apply it.

Chococoa had been a tool; now it was a possession. Nicola too. Nicola was still defiant, he could sense that. She would need a little more bringing along—perhaps he would arrange it so that when she took a shower, blood instead of water would gush out over her; or that when she ordered a gourmet meal and lifted the silver food cover, underneath would be a pile of human fingers. He would not need to harm actually anyone. That would be mere pathetic self-indulgence, he thought, touching a hand unconsciously to his face. A bribe to the right funeral director or morgue attendant would suffice. She would know who arranged it, and what the message was intended to say. And she would do as he asked. That was all that ultimately mattered.

Or so he used to think. The truth is, what really mattered was that more and more he was becoming the ruling head of a multinational conglomerate. His operations kept growing, the size and scope of his power kept expanding, his empire never shrank but only swelled. Terror was a tool he was more comfortable using than most such heads, but in reality he was becoming less and less of a monster and more and more of a manager. A *manager*, he thought. How… bourgeois.

O Ghana, he thought. *Is ruling you my destiny? Was that what the gods gave me when they took away my face?*

The other drug dealers, the criminals and traffickers—they were tiny; petty. Slowly the will of Kwaku was penetrating everywhere: the underworld of Ghana, the businesses of Ghana, the government of Ghana. One day Ghana and Kwaku would become one. And even now he was already passing beyond Ghana, radiating his will ever further.

Where would it ultimately end, when Kwaku *ruled?*

Nicola, he thought. Nicola and her *ethics,* her *world-betterment,* her *goodness,* her *weakness.* Kwaku's face twisted in a caricature of a sneer. Only a higher order of evil could destroy evil. The gods had not taken away Kwaku's face, the gods had given Kwaku life! *Evil men* had burned away Kwaku's face. And one day Kwaku would burn them and all their evil away with them.

And if half the world burned away as well?

Let it burn.

Chapter Five

The Cult

1

Johanna walked into the cutting fields.

The cool sunlight of dawn broke through the leaves and the trees. The workers going to their morning work yawned and scratched. Birds that had never seen or heard of England or Europe cooed and sang. The evaporating memory of a light rain added a mystic gleam to the nature and the air.

She wore khaki pants and a bright green Chococoa T-shirt, and as she walked she slowly lifted her arms straight up into the air, like an Evangelical in ecstasy. Her mouth broke into a brilliant white smile. She began to turn around in circles.

Ghana, she thought. *Ghana, Ghana!* Her heart overflowed.

Behind her, Jacob slapped himself across the face for the fiftieth time.

"*Damn* it!" he sputtered. "There are more bloody damned mosquitoes in this place than Dante's *Inferno!*" He slapped himself again. "*Ow!*"

Johanna laughed. She was lost in memories, lost in

time. She was a four-year-old girl again, sitting on her father's shoulders as he walked into the cocoa fields, singing to her, his machete swinging by his side.

Tata, she thought, *tata*. Papa.

She thought of him now, paralyzed, in bed. Tears came to her eyes, but tears mixed with joy, the joy of coming back once again to the fields of her childhood. What she felt was not pain. It was something sublime.

"OW!" roared Jacob. "God *damn* it!"

She broke into laughter. "I told you to take the bug repellent, idiot."

"It stank!"

She laughed again.

"And it's so *hot!*"

"What are you talking about? It's cool for the fields. It's morning."

"You mean it's going to get *hotter?*"

"That generally happens as the sun gets higher, right?"

Jacob's face turned into a mask of such grief and horror that Johanna thought of Japanese Kabuki. She tried not to laugh again, and share a word of sympathy... but instead she said "Suffer," and cackled.

"*Jojo!*"

A woman in her late forties in a long colorful skirt and a simple headdress lopped a golden cocoa pod off a nearby tree with a single swift professional *chop*, and waved her machete at Johanna in greeting.

"Ofeibea!" cried Johanna. She ran over and they hugged each other.

"Where you been, girl?" said the woman.

"Rainy country!"

They both laughed. Ofeibea looked over at Jacob. "This your man?"

Johanna put a fist to the side of her throat and made out as though she were hanging herself. Both laughed even louder. Johanna jerked a thumb at Jacob. "My brother."

Ofeibea straightened. "A handsome gentleman!" She nodded, as though to royalty. But Jacob was too busy slapping himself on his elbow, forehead and posterior, to look effectively regal.

"I got to talk to the foreman," said Johanna. "I'll be back for lunch, all right? How are things going here? You good? Everything good?"

"Everything?" Ofeibea shrugged. She looked around, not exactly with a smile, not with a frown. "What they say? Same old same old."

"How's the foreman? Treating you right."

Ofeibea smiled. "A good man."

Johanna looked away, and looked back at Ofeibea. "An honest man? Can I trust him?"

Ofeibea laughed. "Who can trust *any* man?"

Johanna noticed Ofeibea's machete and frowned. "Here," she said, giving her Jo's own machete, and taking Ofeibea's. "Cuts better. Less muscle," she said, with a wink, and hugged Ofeibea again. "I'll be back for lunch. Jacob, come on!"

Jacob and Johanna walked on. They passed palmy bright green leaves lolling in a quiet breath of breeze, and then a pile of cocoa pods, brown, yellow, bronze and gold.

"Who was that?" said Jacob.

"Ofeibea. A friend of your father's. And mine. They worked in these fields together." Johanna laughed. "Me too! They had me carry and toss cocoa pods on piles like the one we just saw."

"They made you do child labor?"

Johanna shook her head. "You haven't seen *real* child labor, boy. No, I was just helping. *Tata* made sure no one *made* me do anything. *Ofeibea* made sure too."

"Why'd she call you *Jojo*?"

"In Ghana they name children after the day of the week. *Jojo* means born on Monday too. It's my name."

She looked around, half at her surroundings, half at her memory of her surroundings, and shook the memories off.

She raised the machete. "What do you notice, Mr. Supply Chain Expert?"

"Huh? A machete. That *is* a machete, right?" He slapped himself on the elbow.

Johanna shut her eyes, and sighed.

"Try again."

He looked again, and took it and held it up and turned it around.

"It's still a machete."

"Here's a hint. Touch it. *Feel* it."

Jacob ran his hand over it. He made a brief slash— hoping to castrate a mosquito—and squeezed the handle. He gave it a sniff. He wasn't about to lick it.

"Still nothing?" said Johanna.

He reflected. "It's… it could be sharper?"

Johanna smiled in surprise. "Very good!"

She took the machete and ran her finger along the edge. "Back when Chococoa *had* a supply chain manager, I visited this place and realized in two minutes that sharp blades cut pods fast and clean, and rough blades took more time, and tired workers out. What would you do to improve this aspect of the supply chain, Jacob?"

"I guess I would assign one of the workers here to check the sharpness of every blade before the day began, and sharpen it if the edge was dull."

" 'Dull' is vague. Call it substandard, institute a test—cutting a sheet of paper cleanly, say--and use a cost-effective sharpening device to ensure it reaches your standard."

"OK."

She stopped and placed the blade against the side of Jacob's neck.

"And?"

"Um… Actually have a couple of workers use the sharpened blades? And, uh, get their feedback? And see if it really *does* get the pods cut faster, and improves productivity?"

"And?"

He pursed his lips. "Measure the increased productivity against the time spent sharpening the blades, and the investment in sharpening equipment, to see if it's a genuinely cost-effective advance."

She took the blade away from Jacob's neck.

"Correct. Excellent."

Jacob felt an unexpected thrill of pride. Not that he would let Johanna notice. Though she did.

She held the blade up again. "This," she said, "is substandard."

She tossed the blade to Jacob, who caught it.

"I guess things have changed," he said.

"They're about to change again," said Johanna. *For the better.*

2

The iPhone rang. Or rather, it played the theme from *I Have A Dream* by the Philharmonia Orchestra in full symphony.

"Johanna, darling!" said Benjamin. "How are you? How is Ghana?"

"I need you to do something. Set up a stage-by-stage tour of the supply chain at our factory at Derby for tomorrow."

"I thought you were going to be in Ghana for the next few days?" said Benjamin.

"I am," said Johanna. "But time is short, so *you're* going to take the tour. You won't notice everything I would, but at least you'll be looking. It'll put people on their toes, and you can give me a rough picture. It'll save time when I get there in person. Who knows? You have a fresh pair of eyes, maybe you'll even spot something. Talk to the following people while you're there: Derek Philips, Jack Sweeney, Tariq Fahraji. There's an old guy called Popeye in Engineering. *Definitely* talk to him. Ask them what's going right and what's going wrong. Then report. By phone. The minute you're done. Don't waste time writing it up."

"Now hold on! I have appointments tomorrow!"

"Cancel them."

She hung up.

Benjamin opened his mouth, not sure of what would come out of it. A laugh came out. That girl! A budding Napoleon if ever there was one. She'd have Chococoa invading Russia one day. He could see it now: an army of cocoa pod pickers with her in the lead waving a machete.

He could just ignore her, of course. Or he could go to Naomi and protest. He did have clients to attend to.

But Naomi had made this a priority—and rightly so. Even his father Michael had never been *quite* as obsessive about Chococoa as Johanna, but Chococoa was as much a child of his father as he was, and he owed it to that wonderful man to keep it alive.

And besides—he liked a change now and again. It might be fun.

"Call my secretary," he told his iPhone. The call was placed. "Cancel my appointments for tomorrow, Theresa," he said. "I'm feeling simply *dreadful*."

He waited a moment and called the Derby plant manager.

"Graham here."

"This is Benjamin Anan speaking. I'd like to be given a complete tour of the factory's supply chain tomorrow."

The manager hesitated. "Excuse me, Mr. Anan, but— you're the family *solicitor*, correct?"

"That is correct."

"Is there, uh, something specific that you're looking for? There are some rather technical aspects to operations here…"

"No. I want to see the operation as a whole. That's why I also want a guide who can describe them to me in plain English. Also, I'd like at some point to speak to the following gentlemen," he said, and gave the manager the list.

When he mentioned the elderly fellow in Engineering, the manager broke in laughing.

"Oh! You want to speak to The Cult Of Jo!"

" The 'Cult' Of 'Jo'? "

The manager laughed. "Yeah, that's what we call them around here. Sorry, no disrespect intended, Mr. Anan. Quite the opposite. Your sister had one heck of an impact on some of the people around here a few years ago. *Quite* an impact." Benjamin could hear the smile in the man's tone of voice. "I should let the Cult members talk to you about that, I suppose. Trust me, they'll chat your ear off."

"Do our employee cult worshippers worship any chocolate deities in particular, Mr. Graham? Godiva, perhaps? That's rather heretical, given their employer."

"No, no. Johanna managed to—how can I put it?— well, you'll see. Yes, we can arrange a tour, and a meeting with the people you've mentioned. What's a good time for you to start, Mr. Benjamin?"

"Bright and early at seven?"

"I'll meet you at the factory entrance."

3

After being dismissed by Kwaku, the bodyguard escorted Nicola to the elevator, accompanied her in, and pressed the botton for the ground floor. She stood straight with difficultly; her legs wobbled and when it seemed as though she might fall, the bodyguard put his hand out. She cringed violently, like a beaten dog. The security people whose eyes followed her when she entered now looked at her again—with pity. The guard walked her to the street, then turned away without a word. Nicola stood there, blinking, like a dinghy in the teeming waves of passersby that flowed day and night across the sidewalks of Accra. Eventually the waves pulled her in, and she stumbled along with them for blocks and for more blocks. People noticed her; for her looks, of course, and some because they'd seen her in the papers, and some because of her shattered expression.

After a while she stepped into a small Asian restaurant and went into the bathroom. She sat in one of the stalls. Tears began running down her face, and her breathing grew heavier and heavier. She began screaming uncontrollably, screaming at the top of her lungs. The owner of the establishment, a thin aged Thai woman, eventually rushed in with a cleaver. She opened the door, saw Nicola, and put away her cleaver and grabbed her wrist and slapped her across the face. After the sixth sharp slap, the screaming stopped, and the woman pulled her to the sink, opened water from the faucet, and pushed Nicola's face down and splashed it with water. Nicola twisted at first, but the violent breathing, the shudders, subsided. The woman led her out back, to the alley, and slammed the door behind her. Nicola slipped slowly to the ground and blacked out.

A large rodent woke her as evening approached, tugging at her hair. She shrieked again, but her cry was short and brief, and it fled. She had left her computer and purse at the building, but had no wish to go back there. Ever. What she'd left could be replaced; the data was backed up. Nicola wore an Apple watch and used it to contact a taxi driver. He was there in minutes, and when he asked her where she wanted to go, the answer was, "Anywhere," and then, "No. Take me to the Airport."

She placed another call to the hotel to have her passport and papers delivered there, and when they arrived, she caught the first flight out, regardless of where. She arrived in Ethiopia, then transferred to Moscow, then transferred to Switzerland, than transferred to London, and home.

All along the way, she thought.

I am a rational human being, she thought. *I am a rational human being*.

There is a way out of this situation. There is a logical resolution. There is a way out.

When she finally arrived in the peace and quiet of her elegant Brownstone apartment, she lay on the sofa and wept, covering her face with her hands. Safe at home. Safe. The familiar chairs, fireplace, paintings, filled her with inexpressible joy. She cried. She had cried more in the past day and night than in the last ten years of her life. An unexpected laugh sprang from her lips. She went to the kitchen to make a cup of green tea,

There was a small box of chocolates with a violently red bow waiting on the kitchen table.

She approached it.

There was a note underneath the bow.

Welcome home, Darling.

She pulled at the end of the ribbon. The bow unraveled. She lifted the lid. On an elegant silken bed lay five or six bloody severed fingers, arranged in a ring.

In the center, staring up at her, was a blue eye.

She closed the box.

After a few moments, she took the box to the garbage disposal, and threw it in. The whirring sounds peaked for a moment as they dealt with the bones. She opened the cold water and let it run.

4

"Mr. Benjamin Anan?"

"I am he. And you are?"

"Tariq Fahraji, sir. A pleasure."

The man was young, in his twenties, blonde and blue-eyed, and wore a business suit with all the *élan* of Benjamin himself. Benjamin chastised himself. From the name, he'd been expecting an Arabian-looking figure, or at the very least a turban. *Clichés, clichés,* he thought with a certain embarrassment. Yet he did find the clash of appearance and heritage intriguing.

"Are you a long-time employee with this firm, Mr. Fahraji?"

"I've had the pleasure of working at Chococoa for the past four years, Mr. Anan. Actually it was your sister Johanna who brought me in. She gave a guest talk at London University on supply chain processes that was absolutely riveting. I pestered her with several difficult questions before and during the talk. She liked that, and afterwards gave me her card. Prior to that my main avocation was causing my parents grief. This was in the Maghreb in North Africa. Ten or so years ago they emigrated here as Lebanese Christians. Now they operate a number of mystery book stores dotted throughout Yorkshire."

"Specializing in Agatha Christies, do you mean? Or are the stores just hard to locate?"

He laughed. "A bit of both, frankly. It *is* Yorkshire, you know. But let me show you our operations."

"And after that, will I be initiated into the 'Cult'?"

The blond young man smiled. "I arranged to have eye of newt and toe of frog dropped into our cauldron of blood the moment you called, Mr. Anan. But first things first. Follow me."

Benjamin followed Fahraji through the plant doors, past security, and onto the plant floor. It seemed as much a production factory to Benjamin as any auto manufacturer. His head turned as he took in the huge metallic vats, whirling turrets, robotic arms delving and tweaking items on moving assembly lines, the efficient-looking men in goggles and overalls passing in clumps or driving iron fork-lift vehicles. It could have been almost any technological operation, except for the occasionally overpowering whiffs of chocolate aroma wafting across as pools of the dark liquid poured Niagara-like into tremendous vats just out of sight. A goggled figure drove up in a Plexiglas-shielded jeep, stepped out and waved to Fahraji, and walked off to his next assignment as Fahraji took the driver's seat and gestured to Benjamin to get in. Benjamin did so.

"Here," said Fahraji, handing him a helmet. "Put it on. Regulations."

Fahraji put one on too, and strapped it under his chin.

They pulled away.

"Now the first step in the process is the actual delivery," said Fahraji, pulling up to a set of massive doors. "Once the ships dock, trucks deliver the cocoa beans through those doors. Unfortunately we don't have any arrivals today," he said, "but as you can see from those stacks there on the floor, the sacks of cocoa beans are set down there. Any non-Chococoa materials are set out in that other area for transport."

"Non-Chococoa materials? What do you mean?"

"Apparently our firm has a partnership arrangement with some pharmaceutical manufacturer to save mutual costs on shipping and distribution. You'd have to talk with Finance about that. Our beans, and some minerals and other materials from Ghana used by the manufacturers, are shipped out together and arrive together. Once here they go their separate ways. The other materials go to the manufacturer's space located next to a special section of the factory dedicated to product development. Again, this is all separate from the chocolate production process, so we keep the pharmaceutical materials there till pick-up arrives, so as not to let it get in the way. Anyway, once the beans arrive and are stacked, teams pull up in vehicles not unlike this one, but with long platforms attached. The sacks are placed on the platforms, and taken to the appropriate sections of the factory. There the sacks are opened and the beans are placed on conveyor belts where automated filters again separate the viable beans from any stragglers, and the ones that qualify are then roasted."

"Roasted? Like peanuts?"

"Not like peanuts. Basically, what we do here is take the beans and refine them. A separate section of the facility is dedicated to molding the chocolate into various shapes and bon-bons, and another section to wrapping and packaging the molded units, but this is where the chocolate itself is made. Here machines break down the cocoa beans into cocoa butter and chocolate. We ferment and dry the cocoa beans down to what we call a 'nib' by winnowing and roasting. Then we heat them, and they melt into chocolate liquor. Finally we blend the chocolate liquor with sugar and milk to add flavor."

"Just sugar and milk? What about almonds? Raisins? Crunchy ants for Japanese *gourmands*?"

"We add those too, as appropriate. (Except, I think, for the ants.) After the blending process, the liquid chocolate is either stored, or taken in tanks to the molding area where they'll eventually be poured into molds. Finally, after the well-molded finished items are wrapped and packaged by machines, the completed product is then taken to another set of shipping doors at the opposite end of the plant, where they await transport to distribution centers, stores, cafes, and other points of sale."

Benjamin nodded.

"And of course there are inspectors all along the way taking random samples to ensure quality, compliance with health standards, and so on," said Fahraji

"Of course. So, let's follow the process, section by section."

Fahraji turned the wheel and left the area where the sacks of beans lay stored, and drove over to series of metal vats that looked to Benjamin like a cross between conga drums, atom bomb casings and sieves.

"As I explained, the first thing we do with cocoa beans," said Fahraji, "is roast them."

"Why?"

"It develops the flavor of the bean. And enhances the color as well. Trust me, you wouldn't want to eat the raw bean! A gourmet delicacy it is not. See those machines? The roasting process makes the shells of the cocoa bean brittle, and lets us take off the unappetizing outer shell. The inner cocoa bean, the 'meat,' as it were, is broken into small pieces. We call them cocoa nibs. We pass the nibs through a series of sieves—those things over there—that sort and sift the nibs according to size. That's called 'winnowing.'"

"And then you mash it up and you get chocolate?"

"Not right away, and not always. Did you know that cacao nibs have all the mood-enhancing lipids and chemicals and health benefits of eating dark chocolate, but without the added sugar? They're actually pretty nutritious—high in fiber, protein, and antioxidants. Once upon a time, back before Johanna, and before Nicola, the shells were tossed, all the nibs went on to become packaged chocolate, and that was that. Now that we know there's a market for cocoa nibs as they are, we have a market."

"Now that we've *created* a market, as Nicola might say," interjected Benjamin.

"Yes. Now that we can market the nibs as a health food, some of these nibs go on their own separate organic path as a surprisingly profitable sister product, with less refining needed to boot."

"Thus expanding and profitably modifying the supply chain!"

Fahraji looked at him like a teacher at a promising student. "Exactly. You want to extract as much profit as you can from what you have. We even have ways to make outer shells provide some value, though not, as yet, quite enough. But who knows? Maybe the Research & Development section will have a breakthrough one of these days."

"That's the place next to where they send the pharmaceutical minerals and things."

"Yes. The experimental section is ours—R&D—and the pharmaceutical section is theirs."

"Will we be going there as well?"

Fahraji pouted. "No."

"You look irritated!"

"R&D—the things that go on in any Research and

Development division—are critical to a company, and can potentially impact all its processes. But since some of the things they come up with are proprietary—new formulas and such that we don't want competitors to steal or intuit—the R&D section is off-limits to we *hoi polloi.* Here at Chococoa they take the security clearances and segregation to James Bond levels at times," said Fahraji. "Big Pharma, the pharmaceutical section is even worse. That's not a part of Chococoa, technically. Just rented space. They're very insistent about us *not* violating their space. It can be irksome."

"Yes, but I'm an Anan," said Benjamin, not without a certain flourish of pride. "*And* the firm's solicitor. Surely I can have a look."

"I'm sure *you* can. I can't, nor can anyone on this floor. You'll need clearance directly from Chris in Finance for that."

"Finance?"

Fahraji spread his hands. "Don't ask me to explain. That's the rule, as laid down by the great Nicola herself."

"Strange."

"Security." He shrugged. "All that secrecy goes to people's brains. Too many John Le Carre novels, I suppose."

"You sound rather critical."

"You're here to examine the supply chain process, I understand. Well, as Johanna used to say, a good supply chain process is a *clear* one, transparent and verifiable by multiple parties. If you can see what you're doing, you can see if it works and if it makes sense. If it's a black box, who knows if your assets are being well spent or well directed?"

Benjamin nodded, making a mental note.

Fahraji returned to the subject at hand, driving slowly past the sieves, pointing out various features that Benjamin did not quite grasp, but whose basic purpose and sequence was clear to him once explained. He nodded, and when Fahraji noticed that his guest appeared to have understood things to this point, he drove on.

They turned the corner, and came upon an expanse of vast rollers turning in what appeared to be the feature products of a Jacuzzi showroom.

"And these are?"

"Grinders," said Fahraji, "and this is grinding: the process by which cocoa nibs are ground into liquor."

"Liquor?"

"Cocoa liquor, to be precise. Sometimes we call it cocoa mass as well. I believe you know it as 'unsweetened chocolate'?

"So this crushes the beans all up into a kind of peanut butter consistency and it comes out as unsweetened chocolate."

"Well, roughly. To be exact, it isn't so much the crushing as the heat. There's a large amount of fat in cocoa nibs, and when heat is applied, the fat melts. As it does so, the cocoa nibs go from being granular and dry, to becoming liquefied. The physical pressure helps too, of course. You can't just put it in a pan, or use a blowtorch. Believe me, we've experimented, though not *that* foolishly."

"And once you've got unsweetened chocolate, it's nearly done?"

"Far from it." Fahraji turned the wheel and headed up and to the left to a new bank of machinery. "See those?" he said. "This is where we add new items to the base cocoa liquor. Cocoa butter, for instance. Sugar. Milk."

"Bottled milk?"

"When it comes to milk chocolate, we add powdered whole milk, or in some cases sweetened condensed milk. There hasn't been a good deal of innovation coming out of Research & Development lately in this area—or any area," he grumbled, "—but once upon a time we experimented with goat's milk, almond milk, coconut milk—all sorts of things. Cheese. Vodka."

"You're joking."

"Some of the experiments *were* a joke. But as Johanna said—sorry, I'm getting ahead of myself."

"Go right ahead!"

He smiled. "Johanna used to say that a good supply chain process wasn't just about taking a set of good processes and running them into the ground. It wasn't always about just being good, or staying good, or even getting better. Sometimes you had to be willing to be *bold*, to risk being willing to fail, because sometimes failure could teach you more than success. Some of the things we tried didn't work, but we learned something new every time, and it helped Chococoa build up a product line that was second to none."

" 'Was' ?"

Fahraji frowned.

"Don't misunderstand me, Mr. Anan. This company makes a fine product. World class. It's just not as… *ambitious* as it was. Not as determined to take the lead. A few years ago we wanted to make the best chocolate in the world and to make the world know it. Since then— well, frankly, the product hasn't evolved, and the PR about how great we are is getting to sound a little tired. I hope you don't mind my bluntness."

"Not at all. Though I'd like to know more about the reasons for your opinions."

"Oh, the Cult will have no problem sharing them, I'm sure!"

"So our product hasn't 'evolved.' How so?"

"The next stage will explain."

The vehicle passed down yet another factory floor, pausing for other traffic and passing parties of workingmen and women and checklist-bearing sub-managers.

It came to a sharp halt. Fahraji pointed at stern walls of new machinery. They looked to Benjamin like inverted rocket boosters. He wondered, absurdly, whether the mechanisms he was looking at really did anything at all, or whether they were all just masterpieces of papier-mâché fakery. Did Tariq Fahraji and the Cult of Jo regularly sneak out to Hershey's or God knows where, buy up their chocolate, and bring the lot down here to change the labels and double the price?

He shook his head. *You're going on like this because you don't really know what all these things do,* he realized, and he rued the insight. In the courtroom he was masterful, and he handled the firm's business documentation masterfully too; but he had gotten out of touch with the day-to-day operations of his own family's business. His father's business. He felt embarrassed—and determined to master this area too.

"We only make three basic kinds of product now," says Tariq. "After the processes you've already seen, we refine the blend further, taking the size of the added milk and sugar particles to different levels of smoothness, and blending in cocoa powder, butter, liquor. It produces different kinds of *covertures*—chocolates—but the differences are subtle. Basically there's only white chocolate, dark chocolate and milk chocolate. White chocolate is made up of cocoa liquor, cocoa butter, sugar, milk (or milk powder), lecithin, an emulsifier, and Vanilla. Milk chocolate is the same thing, plus cocoa powder. Dark chocolate keeps the added cocoa powder, but eliminates the milk, or milk powder. It's that simple."

"And that's it?"

"By and large. After the blends are done, we take them to the adjacent molding and packaging divisions. The chocolate is poured into the molds, it cools, and then the finished molded products are wrapped, boxed and sent off to distribution."

Fahraji looked at his watch, "We have a few minutes. Would you like to look over anything here again?"

"Not at the moment."

Benjamin wished he'd had the foresight to bring an engineer along. Perhaps that Popeye fellow. Benjamin sensed that a sixteenth of an inch difference in a machine part here, a variation of a half a degree there, would shave pennies off the processes he'd witnessed, pennies that would accumulate into millions over the span of a decade. No doubt that was what Johanna would have wanted him to spot. But he could no more see it than Fahraji could fathom a deceased Victorian's codicil.

"Next stop," said Fahraji, "The Cult!"

5

I am a rational human being, thought Nicola. *I am a rational human being.*

It was a mantra she repeated in times of stress. She had repeated it almost every day since returning from Ghana. Sometimes every hour.

Now she sat alone in the Board Room at Chococoa's offices. The room was silent. All her appointments for the moment were cancelled. She had told her staff here to tell everyone that she had had a severe allergic reaction to something she'd eaten in Ghana, and had been isolated for a day by her physician and had had to return home. Everyone accepted it. Now she had come back to the firm's offices. The staff were gone, the offices were closed, her fear had drained away, there was not a sound to be heard. She was under control.

She could think clearly now. She was normal. She was cold.

Reason it out. What was the situation? What was the logical next step?

She could go to the police. In which case Kwaku might or might not murder her. Probably, he would.

She could work for Kwaku. That was not acceptable either. He was obviously a monster. A killer. It was not the inhumanity of his features that repelled her. It was the inhumanity within. It was better to be dead than to facilitate the actions of that kind of—that animal, that *demon*.

She could wash her hands of it all. Quit. Would

Kwaku allow her to walk away? Unlikely, but possible. And it would not stop him. Her departure would at best only inconvenience him, momentarily disrupt his money laundering. At worst, her successor would follow the trail of funding through the Freedom For The Children organization and end up in the same room with Kwaku. Nothing would really change.

She could partially, selectively, wash her hands of it. She could let Kwaku's activities proceed and have no direct involvement. She had had no knowledge of it when she walked into his office. Kwaku was a cancer within Chococoa, but perhaps, handled with care, it would not spread. Things would operate as before, the only difference being that she would be aware now of his operations. Did that really matter? She could continue bringing positive attention to Chococoa, and present it as a model of ethical business practice.

After all, Kwaku's operations went on in parallel to Chococoa's. Their core business was untouched. And beside, a model didn't have to *be* ethical to be perceived as ethical. Even a false image could inspire.

But perhaps she was wrong. If what Kwaku had told her was the truth, he *had* reduced child trafficking, he *had* built schools and fed children, he *had* removed criminals as evil as himself from the face of the earth. True, he had done it to advance his own evil purposes, but Good achieved inadvertently was still Good.

Could she steer him even further in that direction? It was not an impossibility.

A crooked smirk disfigured her lips. Nor was it a probability.

She sank her face into her hands. What to do?

Wash her hands of it.

She called Chris. It was the dead of evening. He picked up, groggy, disoriented and puzzled.

"Nicola—?"

"Chris. You're aware of the relationship we have with Freedom For The Children, correct?"

"Huh? I mean, like—sure. I guess."

"I'm putting you in complete charge of it. Anything they want—give it to them."

"Me? Anything?"

"I don't want this on my plate. It's yours. Just keep me informed. Let me know if they ask for anything new or unusual."

She hung up.

Now Chris' hands would be dirty, not hers.

Liar, she thought. *Coward. You've made your hands even dirtier.*

Chris's hands were already dirty, just as hers were. He'd handled all the cash flow from the 'charity' to date. The only difference was that he remained ignorant. His ignorance shielded him. Nicola's knowledge degraded her. This way she might not be *actively* involved. But she was still morally culpable.

She closed her eyes.

And another option came to her. She could let Chococoa collapse.

Slowly. Plausibly.

After all, she was not the firm's owner, but as its manager she could modulate its fortunes as she pleased. There could be a buyout. A fire. A bankruptcy. Regulatory violations leading to a shutdown.

Businesses fail. Chococoa could fail too.

No Chococoa, no conduit or income source for Kwaku.

If Kwaku suspected, that would be the end of Nicola Cavalcanti. A slow and horrifically painful end.

And it was not really a *solution.* Kwaku's operation was a parasite that would only find some other host.

It would never end till someone put a bullet through Kwaku's head.

Or till she put a bullet through her own.

She was a rational human being. She would consider all the options. Till acting on one.

6

Fahraji nodded and turned the vehicle left, right, left, down one ramp, up one path, and finally came to a halt at a room in some cranny far from the machinery.

It had a large handwritten sign on the door that said, "Go Away!"

Fahraji got out and opened the door.

"After you, sir."

Benjamin walked in. It was too small to be a break room, and too casual to be a conference room. Two men were seated around a table having coffee.

"Where's Popeye?" said Fahraji.

"The Disco," said one of the two men.

"Seriously."

"Beats me."

"You did tell him who this is, right?"

"If Popeye's elsewhere, it's for a good reason."

Fahraji frowned, but then nodded in agreement. The look on his face said that the comment was probably true.

"Well, you can meet with him later on. No need to waste time waiting." Fahraji cleared his throat. "Gentlemen! This is Benjamin Anan, brother to The Oracle! He has come among us to hear The Word."

The two men broke into whistles and applause, and so did Fahraji.

"Mr. Anan," he smiled, indicating the two with a wave of his hand. "Behold the Cult of Jo!"

The men waved their hands hello.

"Er... Blessed Be She," said Benjamin.

"He feels the Spirit," said the larger of the two men. He was large and bulky, with florid cheeks, a sweeping handlebar moustache, and a Dublin brogue. "Jack Sweeney, sir, at your service."

The other man was tall and slim and geeky. He had thick eyeglasses and for some reason made Benjamin think of a science fiction writer. "Derek Philips, Mr.

Anan," he intoned, in as upper-class a Prince Charles accent as Benjamin had ever heard.

"Gentlemen, call me Benjamin, please."

"Benjamin," explained Fahraji, "is here for a reason. It appears that Johanna has been tasked with doing a supply chain analysis on operations, from Ghana through our distribution channels to our customers."

Both men brightened visibly.

"Well, it's about damn time," said Sweeney. Philips grinned, exposing teeth with a surprising gap here and there, a grin as unexpectedly charming as a three-year old's.

"So what are you gentlemen all about, anyway?"

"Derek? You're more lucid than Sweeney ever was," said Fahraji, smiling. "Take the lead."

"Well, Mr. Anan—Benjamin—it's nothing very grandiose. Back five or six years ago, your sister graduated with her MBA and various certifications and started working here. She really made an impression."

"And how!" added Sweeney.

"Before Johanna, the operation here was *good*, everything *functioned*, chocolate was made and packaged and shipped, and things were profitable, but they weren't—"

Philips searched for the right word.

"They weren't *interesting*. They weren't thoughtful. You had a clear job to do and you did it and went home. You didn't think about the operation as a whole, or ways to improve it. Things here were like a machine, and the people here were like parts. The machine worked, but it was just a job, like any other job. You know… a little, well, boring. Johanna, on the other hand, was fresh out of college and wanted to transform everything from the bottom up."

Sweeney nodded. "What an evangelist she would have made!"

"She poked her nose into everything, talked to everyone, never stopped asking us questions. She just had this *determination* to make Chococoa something legendary. Really, she was amazing."

"And step one was to get the workforce educated," added Sweeney. "She started giving free talks about supply chains and *kaizen* and the Four P's and the Seven W's and—"

"The 'Seven W's'?" said Benjamin, raising his left eyebrow.

All three men laughed. "Sound off!" called Sweeney.

"Adapt The Supply Chain to the Customer's Needs," cried Fahraji, saluting smartly.

"Customize the Logistics Network," said Philips

"Align Demand Planning Across The Supply Chain," barkcd Sweeney.

"Differentiate Products Close to The Customer," continued Philips.

"Outsource Strategically!" shouted Sweeney.

"Develop IT that Support Multi-Level Decision Making," intoned Philips.

"Adopt Both Service and Financial Metrics!" concluded Fahraji.

All three applauded and laughed again.

Benjamin looked at them all in complete confusion.

"We're sorry, Mr. Anan. I guess we sound silly. It's anything *but* silly, really. Johanna kept giving talks and lessons and sat down with people throughout the floor, one on one, about how—about how everything worked! About how each operation integrated with each other, about how interdependent we all are here. We began to see it—to connect up. To see how what we were doing fit with everything else."

"More than that," added Sweeney. "She got us thinking about how to do things better. She kept at us all the time, soliciting input. 'How can we make this safer?' 'How can we make this more efficient?' It wasn't top-down orders from The Boss. It was The Boss asking us how *we* could make it all function better. For them and for us. How to make things easier!"

Fahraji nodded emphatically. "She got us thinking."

Philips nodded too. "There's a difference between doing a job and *thinking* about doing your job. Thinking about how to do things better. How others could do things better. Paying attention, *creatively*, instead of just going through the motions. Coming to work just became a lot more... interesting."

Sweeney agreed. "She was just so damned passionate about it. It was infectious."

"Mr. Anan—Benjamin," said Philips. "Have you ever heard about *kaizen*?"

"No," **replied** Benjamin.

They all rolled their eyes.

Sweeney shook his head. "Johanna would *talk our ears off* about *kaizen*."

"*Kaizen*," said Philips, "is a Japanese philosophy. They use it in business. The idea is to create continuous improvement based on small, positive, ongoing changes. Not big radical changes. Small improvements from the bottom up." He rubbed his chin. "You know, I used to waste time every morning looking for my shoes. I'd slip them off when I got home as the spirit moved me, and in the morning I could never find them. 'Apply *kaizen!*' said Johanna. I thought about it, went home, and put seven sets of shoes right by my bedside. In the morning, every day of the week, at least one pair was always there! Problem solved.

"You may not think that is any great accomplishment, but imagine a workplace like this one with everyone thinking about how to make things work just a little better in some small way. Eventually the little things add up, and things get better in big ways. After a while, and after Johanna's talks started sinking in, cramped areas became uncramped, injuries on the work floor stopped happening, tools you needed were right at hand instead of halfway across the factory." He lifted up a coffee cup. "*Now*, the coffee's always hot and always waiting! Little things just got better. Even our home lives got better."

Sweeney and Tariq nodded.

"Anyway, as for the 'Cult'," resumed Philips—well, some of us just got very taken with your sister, and where she seemed to be taking things. We got involved. Personally. It wasn't a paid function."

"Well, she *did* have that thing where she gave prizes for a really good idea," recalled Sweeney.

"That's true," observed Philips. "But that wasn't the main thing. You just want to work in a place where things operate more efficiently and where your ideas are heard. Where you get to use your brain. And so after a while a real fan base began building up around your sister. We'd all meet down here and discuss things, and we still do."

Benjamin had a sudden realization. "You people are Johanna's 'Shadow Government'. She's gone, but you're keeping an eye out of things here for her, aren't you?"

"I wouldn't put it *that* way," said Sweeney.

"Especially not to Nicola," added Fahraji.

"We don't have any power or any authority, Mr. Anan," said Philips. "We're not even managers. We're engineers. Except for Popeye, and he's—what the hell is he, Jack?"

"I think he's a consultant."

"Anyway. Johanna built up a kind of a culture here—a Supply Chain *mindset*, or Kaizen mindset, or whatever you want to call it, and it's persisted. We still get together and talk about the company, the floor operations, and how things are going. How to make the dumb things go away or become less of a pain in the butt. How to make things go easier and quicker. Johanna keeps in touch. Except that we haven't heard from her in a while."

"Well, gentlemen, she definitely wants to hear from *you*. She mentioned you three specifically. I'm sure she would welcome a call. She asked me to come down to give things a rough look-over, but clearly your input would be more incisive than what I might casually notice. So. Tell me—how *is* the company. How are things going, operationally?"

They looked at one another.

It was not very positive look. Nor was it especially negative. Jack Sweeney swept a hand across his moustache contemplatively, and took the lead this time.

"I think we'd all agree that nothing is outright falling apart, but that things are kind of stagnant. That continual improvement Derek mentioned? It's pretty much come to a halt. I mean—sorry for sounding egotistical, but any improvements in production now are coming from us. Literally, the three of us in this room, and Popeye. We're still looking at things the way Johanna used to, and when we see something that could be done better, we mention it, and sometimes the people doing it take our input. And sometimes they just don't care, and neither do the people managing them. It's almost weird. It's like there's no driving force to stay competitive anymore. Johanna left, and soon after everything just rolled to a halt. We're not in *bad* shape—"

"Yet," observed Fahraji.

"—but we're just going along, same as before, day after day. It feels like the shop is just sitting here rusting."

Benjamin's head tilted. "Why?"

Sweeney shrugged. "Near as we can tell, just plain lack of interest."

"From whom?"

"Nicola," interjected a raspy voice behind Benjamin.

Behind him was an old fellow in blue jeans and a checked shirt that looked as though he'd stepped out of a cowboy movie, complete with dust. He looked as though he were in his eighties, and walked with a cane. He wore a red baseball cap that bore the legend, "Make Chococoa Great Again."

Grins passed across the faces of the Cult of Jo.

"You're late, grandpa!"

"Did you bring fresh coffee?"

"Where've you been, you old goat?"

"Out chasing schoolgirls," rasped the old man. "Who's the guy in the suit? Your ex-wives' attorney?"

"We finally got an undertaker ready to measure you for that coffin."

"If he's looking for dead meat, he can start with your brains," said the new arrival. "Or maybe a few of your *smaller* organs."

The Cult hooted.

The old man turned and held his hand out to Benjamin. "Popeye," he said. "You must be Jo's baby brother. Fine young woman. She speaks well of you."

The Cult started up again. Popeye gave them the finger.

"Er... she speaks well of you as well, Mr., uh, 'Popeye.' Forgive me, is that your real name?"

"No."

"What is it, may I ask?"

"Vyvienne Ezekiel Blyth-Palliser. The Fourth."

Benjamin nodded. "Say no more."

"Why the delay, Pops?" said Sweeney. "Seriously."

"One of the sieves was malfunctioning. Held up the whole array. They were sending out to get some kind of damned ultrasonic device to figure what the problem was. Saw the same damn thing when I was at Hershey's in '98. Had a kid go get a bottle of cider vinegar and poured it around the bearing joint." He snapped his fingers. "Cleared it right up."

"You were formerly at Hershey's, Mr. Blyth-Palliser?"

"Please. Popeye's fine. Hershey's, Nestlé, Godiva, the Ferrero Group, Meiji, Lindt & Sprugli, Perfetti Van Melle, Haribo, Arcor, Mars, Toblerone. I've worked everywhere."

Fahraji held out a chair for the new arrival. "Thanks, Tariq," he smiled. "You're wondering what a decrepit ruin like myself is doing working here, is that correct, Mr. Anan?"

"Benjamin, please. And—no disrespect intended— but you *do* seem to have reached retirement age."

"Retirement is for the dead," noted Popeye crisply. "Not for the brain-dead, obviously," he said, tossing a glance at Sweeney.

Then he looked with a serious expression at Benjamin.

"Your sister has several good ideas about what's needed to make a company tick," said Popeye. "One of them is experience. She said that every company needs what she called a 'real-world storyteller,' if not a couple of them. And a real-world storyteller is someone who's been around, seen a lot, and can pass it along to others. Like those people having the sieve issues. That was a simple fix. Simple! You just had to have been around long enough to have seen it and remember it. Problem is, nowadays once you're in your forties, the company gets rid of you. 'We need young blood!' Except young blood doesn't know what to do, and you need to train young blood from scratch, while what they need to be doing gets put on hold. Johanna figured an old coot like myself could prove valuable input now and again."

"Like today."

He shrugged. "It's just common sense. *Kaizen*, matching supply chain practice against theory and vice versa, leveraging strategic assets, benchmarketing the competition. Looking at every step in the process from planting the cocoa trees to taking an online order, and asking yourself how to make it better. What works now, what works for others, what similar situations you can call up to illuminate the existing one. It all adds up."

"And what situations *can* you recall that will illuminate Chococoa's situation?"

"Oh, there are hundreds of examples, Mr. Anan. Take Kodak! World's leading film company. Then, when digital and Fuji started coming in, they did nothing. 'We don't do digital. It's a fad. Film and film alone is what we do. No need to make a change.' Next stop: bankruptcy."

"Is that the issue here?"

He pursed his lips. "Not entirely. It's a big part of it. Something happened to Nicola three years ago. She was never much interested in the supply chain or product development, but she didn't oppose it. If Johanna sent up a proposal that made sense, she'd accept it. Then Johanna left, and boom. Everything stopped. And Nicola keeps *spending money*, and spending it on PR and on those charities of hers, which are just another form of PR. Nothing on maintenance, innovation, upkeep. She also keeps wasting money on R&D but nothing ever comes out." He turned his head. "What's that Seventh W, boys?"

"Adopt Both Service and Financial Metrics," chanted the rest of the Cult in unison.

"R&D isn't supplying any services, except maybe to that shipping partner, and we don't even know that. Financially it's chewing up funds, screwing around generating data, but not turning it into anything—not giving back. She should just cut out all that putzing around. She doesn't even give it any attention. We old folks have seen it all before. It's Kodak all over again."

"And Chris can enlighten me about that? About her PR spending? About the Research and Development division?

Popeye snorted. "Chris looks, sounds, acts like and is, a complete weasel. Good luck getting any straight talk out of him. He doesn't even have a finance degree. He used to be a geek—still is—and Nicola brought him in originally to make sure all the financial data was digitized and secure. The previous head of Finance, Richard Harley, died in a car accident and—God knows why!—Nicola kept Chris on as head of the department. It's like putting Sweeney her in charge of the Fornication Department. You need to get someone who has experience!"

Sweeney leaned forward. "That's right on the dot. Except for my vast romantic experience, of course. Nicola ignores what's happening on the floor, doesn't replace things, doesn't innovate, but *does* send a notable amount of money to the Research Department, which never seems to produce anything anymore. And a *fortune* on advertising and public relations."

Philips raised his hand. "Boys, be fair. Sometimes

R&D results do take time, and sometimes they don't pan out. It happens. And Nicola *does* know PR in and out, and that *did* set the company on absolute fire in terms of profitability a few years ago."

Popeye cocked an eye in Benjamin's direction. "You know her David Ogilvy story, right? Ogilvy was this leading Ad Agency guy in the USA in the 50's. One day he has a friend over and gives him a glass of cheap brandy, the worst possible, and asks him to taste it because Ogilvy is wondering if he should take the cheap label on as a client. His friend drink it, screws up his face, and goes Ugh! So Ogilvy takes the bottle away, goes in the back, finds a bottle of *Hine Triomphe Cognac*—$1,000 a bottle—pours the good stuff into another bottle and fills the super-expensive bottle with the cheap label brandy. He goes back to the guy and says, "To make up for having you drink that cheap brandy, I'm going to share a glass of the exquisite world-classic century-old *Hine Triomphe*." He pours the *exact same cheap brandy* out of the bottle, the guy takes a sip, and he nearly floats up to Heaven. Best brandy he's ever tasted! Ogilvy concludes breathlessly: '*He is tasting the advertising!*' "

"Well," concluded Popeye, "that's Nicola in a nutshell. She thinks that if our factory produces absolute crap *but* people think its high-quality, ethical, gourmet confectionary, an aristocratic treat that's the chocolate of choice for the Royal Family and the Rothschilds, it's game over and we make a fortune. Nothing else matters but convincing the public that it's absolutely terrific, like no other chocolate. As for the actual quality, the production process, the chain of supply and distribution—well, you can hire people to do that, but really it doesn't matter very much. It's what they *think* of it, not what it *is*.

"And that kind of attitude was fine, *when* the people overseeing the production process were supply chain expert specialists like Johanna. Then people not only *thought* it was the best, it *was* the best. It was the best of both worlds. The only people overseeing it now, really, are the people in this room. We're not official or anything, but we're respected. We make our opinions known. People listen. But it's not like having someone near the top actively facilitating things. I swear, sometimes Nicola acts like she *wants* the company to go under."

"Ah, Popeye, come on," said Sweeney. "Why would she?"

Benjamin placed his hands together in thought.

"Gentlemen, are you telling me that the supply chain process here in the Derby factory is essentially sound, although it could do with improvement?"

The Cult looked at one another. Popeye spoke for them.

"It's not as simple as that," he said, "but yes."

"Nonetheless the company is facing… certain strains."

"I know," concurred Popeye.

Benjamin had the distinct impression that he did know and in close detail. "So what are the problems, as you see them?"

Again, Popeye spoke. "Partly it's nothing we can control. Bad weather in Africa, less cocoa beans grown, supply down, futures prices acting nutty. Political mess over the EU, financial markets are worried, banks raising interest rates. What we *can* control is the amount of money Nicola is pouring into advertising and public relations—really, into her charities."

"Cutting funds from charities makes a bad impression on the buying public."

"Going bankrupt makes a worse one," **grunted** Popeye

"I'd replace Chris with a *real* financial person," **added** Fahraji.

"Do you think he's embezzling?" asked Benjamin.

"He's just weird," observed Popeye. "He puts out these reports. No overviews, no summaries. Pure numbers buried in techie gobbledygook. I honestly don't think he knows what the complete financial picture is."

"The company needs someone with a banking background," said Philips. "Possibly get us better terms on our loans."

"Agreed," said Popeye. "And someone needs to go through the R&D Department top to bottom. That place is a black hole. We have no idea what they're doing. That's unacceptable. There has to be some transparency."

"Someone needs to go through the Pharma section next door. What the hell are they doing in there? They act like B-movie CIA. Nobody has any idea!"

Benjamin frowned. If only in his head, he needed to formulate a proposal to take to Johanna. Naomi had given only Johanna the authority to act unilaterally and decisively.

But the decisive actions were clear. Marketing might be over-funded and its use of funds misspent, but that was a judgment call, and there was no mystery about it. R&D and pharmaceutical partner's operations *were* mysteries. Black holes. That needed illumination.

Benjamin looked at the others.

"Gentlemen. I propose we visit and thoroughly investigate the R&D division," he said, "--and raid Big Pharma."

Chapter Six

Overviews

1

Johanna swung her machete. It helped her think. She struck the base of the pod hanging on the cocoa tree, and severed it with one swift clean *plop*.

Her iPhone rang. She unclipped it from her belt.

"Johanna?"

"Benjamin. What's up?"

"Just calling to update."

"No real need. I've already talked to a few people there."

"Ah, your little shadow government. *The Cult!*"

Benjamin could hear her smile. "Now that's an exaggeration and you know it."

"I know it, and I admire it regardless. I have to confess, after you left I thought things would go into a decline."

"They have gone into a decline."

"Not operationally. At least, not much. Your carefully seeded little group seems to have kept things humming. Smart. Bravo, Jo!"

"Benjamin, businesses will never completely

automate, and you know why? Because robots don't *innovate*. They don't come up with *idea*s. People aren't robots: they think. They imagine. And once you get people on the team thinking, they never go back. Using your brain, figuring about how to make things around you function better, is much, much more interesting than showing up at work and going through the same mindless motions. It's part of management's job to foster that."

"Spoken like an evangelist!"

"Why not? Remember what Taiichi Ohno of Toyota once said? Something like, "People don't go to Toyota to 'work,' they go there to 'think'. Exactly right. Why *not* make the work easier and more interesting?" *Exactly* right. The approach works, Benjamin. Don't pat *me* on the back, pat Pops and all the rest of them. Those guys get it."

"You all deserve pats on the back."

"You didn't call just to say that."

"No. Your friend Fahraji took me step-by-step through the chocolate processing, and later Jack Sweeney took me through the part where they mold and package the chocolate. Amazing, I might add. What precision! The machinery operates almost like a ballet. It was *dazzling*. Only..."

"Only?"

"Only—well, I didn't have much to contribute. I kept asking Sweeney and everyone whether we could improve this and that, and there was an interesting answer or two—which I assume you've already gotten."

"Of course," said Johanna. "I call the guys and the guys call me, and into the simulation model it goes. Granted, there *are* some improvements we could make."

"So I gathered from my own talks with them. But not, I fear, many."

Johanna, on the other end, was silent. "That's correct--unfortunately. There *are* things we could do that *would* make an impact. A big one. Things we need to start on right away. But the results wouldn't be in for months. Years."

"And we don't have months or years."

"No," said Johanna. "We don't."

"I'm sorry, Johanna. I'm an attorney, not a technician or an efficiency expert. I didn't see anything that your friends haven't already seen."

"I didn't send you on the tour to *see* anything at all," said Johanna.

"Then why did you send me?"

"To *be* seen," said Johanna. "To have a member of the family *be* there, on the floor, *doing* something, *talking* to them, like Dad used to do. That bitch Nicola hasn't shown up on the work floor *once*."

"Jo, please. Come on, you know that's not fair."

Johanna ground her teeth. Men. They always cut eye candy like Nicola slack.

But Benjamin was right. She was not being fair. She and Nicola could not have more opposed views on how to run a business. But as far as Johanna knew, Nicola had no personal life, no vices, no indulgences. She wasn't even rude. Just cold. But likability wasn't the issue. Johanna couldn't deny that Nicola's dedication to the firm seemed total. She even had to admit that, in her own area, Nicola got results.

But to Nicola everything was all facade, all hits and Likes and superstar 'leadership'. To Johanna, the business meant production, *doing it*, shoulder to shoulder with those on the ground.

"Ben, trust me, it makes a difference—a *big* difference—to have one of us on the floor looking into operations. Getting feedback. Listening."

Benjamin nodded. "Understood. I think I might be more helpful, however, contacting the banks and seeing if we might get better terms."

"Worth doing, yes. Go right ahead and do it," said Johanna. "But before you do, there's still something I'd like you to do at the plant."

"What is that?"

"I want you to do a surprise tour of the R&D section. Both divisions. Including the part we rent out to the partner company."

Benjamin laughed. "Great minds think alike!"

"What do you mean?"

"That's just what I'm preparing to do. With the help of your cult worshippers."

"You're kidding," said Johanna. She was surprised. She thought of solicitors as people who kept things *from* happening, not people who actually did things. "What got that idea into *your* head?"

"The Cult reported that the supply chain was fundamentally sound—well, increasingly *dilapidated*, really, but sound enough for the time being."

Johanna nodded. "Same impression I'm getting here in Ghana."

"But that there were a couple of puzzles. Operations that were draining funds with little result, like R&D, or that were just blanks, like that Pharma partnership sharing our shipping and distribution and using our space. Well, you can't get the information you need if you don't look, so I said, gentlemen—let's stage a raid!"

"That's a surprisingly bold move, Benjamin. Good for you. I'm impressed."

"I wanted to clear it with you first."

"I want to clear it with *you* first," said Johanna. "You're the solicitor. We can examine our own facilities, but what about the Pharma section. That's an independent company."

"I've reviewed the contracts. We can't inspect casually, but we *do* have the right to inspect their premises if we receive information that there may be health or environmental issues. "

"I'll email you the anonymous tip tomorrow."

"And we do need to notify them. But the contract does not specifically say we need to do it beforehand. Mind you: we *may* be facing a law suit, and they may respond negatively, even dissolve our relationship."

"In a month there'll be nothing left to sue, unless they want to sue the new buyer. As for the relationship, I can't get enough information from Chris even to say that we're breaking even on it. Something is *off* about the whole thing. It's like they're piggybacking along on our supply chain and facilities and distribution, and who are they? Ben, that place is a black box. I've been trying to get Chris to get me details, but it's like pulling teeth. All I get is gobbledygook and a promise that he'll get a report in after he does something-or-other for Johanna. There's *no time.* If it's some kind of useless parasite feeding on our supply chain—or worse--I need to know, and know now. We need to know what's going on in there."

"So you're good with it? You want us to do the raid?"

"Don't call it that. Take a page from Johanna. Call it a safety inspection."

Benjamin chuckled. "I'm glad you're open to a lesson from the loyal opposition. Nicola does have a few strengths, you know."

Johanna grunted.

"Jo—," said Benjamin. "What did you mean when you said 'Or worse'?"

Johanna frowned. She'd said too much.

Because I think it's an illicit drug operation, Johanna wanted to shout.

Except she didn't think that. She suspected it one moment, dismissed it the next. It was the only explanation, and it was impossible. Nicola involved in international drug smuggling was like Mr. Spock standing on a street corner, wearing gold chains and a yellow fedora with a purple feather, selling cocaine. Unthinkable.

But it all *fit.* The mysterious security. The pointless deal with the partner company to share the shipping. (Ridiculously, the company called itself 'Big Pharma' with some initials tailing after.) The 'preparation' those materials got—without oversight—when they arrived in the Chococoa facilities in Derby. The way they piggybacked on Chococoa's European distribution. It added up. They were moving drug materials to Europe under the cover of Chococoa, cutting it in the labs, and moving it out once again under the cover of Chococoa.

Angrily, Johanna slashed her machete into the cocoa tree, where it stayed stuck. Chococoa. *Ethical* chocolate. If Johanna's suspicions were right, not only would the company be ruined, so would the family's reputation. Her father's good name. The business might not only be shut down, family members might be facing prison.

God. She put her hand over her face. Things just seemed to be going from worse to worse.

But the partnership was an anomaly in the chain. A glaring anomaly. There was no reason for it to be there. What the Cult said about Derby held for operations in Ghana too. Nicola had made no improvements in production, but also no changes. Things had aged and rusted to a degree—all right, a *large* degree—and adaptations and updates were needed here and there, but by and large things remained solid. Nicola operated— *presided* over—a sound operation.

What had hurt Chococoa were unexpected changes in the world market. Murderously ill-timed fluctuations in futures prices. Uncertainty over Brexit. But circumstances like those were out of Johanna's hands, and if Chococoa's operations themselves were basically sound, but *still* failing, there was nothing Johanna could do, not in the short term.

So far the only thing that didn't make sense was the arrangement with 'Big Pharma'. It had evolved after Johanna's departure, and, in supply chain terms, added space and logistics complications but, so far as she knew, no particular value. And it was hard to know because Nicola, with her monomaniacal focus on public relations and public perceptions, directed all questions on the subject to Chris. And Chris was all bumbling obfuscation. A blank wall.

It *nagged* at her.

"Look, I've been trying to look into our shared shipping operations here, and the company won't even talk to me. Something's going on. I need to know what's going on in there because I *need to know*, all *right?*"

"Well, fine," said Benjamin, in a slight huff at her tone. "Whatever. We're agreed, so how do you propose we go about it?"

"I called Pops, and he knows someone who ran R&D for Hershey's once upon a time."

"Another octogenarian?"

"He can be older than the pyramids provided he knows his stuff. And Popeye assures me he does. Chemistry Ph.D. and everything. If there's anything out of the ordinary going on in the Pharma section, or in R&D, this guy will spot it."

"OK."

"Get together with him. Take Naomi along if you have to get in. Bring smartphones, take pictures, samples. Find out what the hell they're doing in there."

"*Samples* could be a violation of our agreement," said Benjamin. "As I understand it, we're partnering with a firm to ship material—herbs and minerals in their case, I believe—and we're allowing them do some lab work on it at our facility prior to it's being distributed. Those processes are almost certainly proprietary. A safety inspection is one thing. If we walk in on them and *sample* their proprietary products, *record* their operations, we are assured of facing a serious lawsuit."

"We're facing bankruptcy already," said Johanna. "If we go out of business, what's left to take?"

They were both silent.

"Should I inform Nicola?" said Benjamin. "Chris?"

"*No*," said Johanna, flatly. "Not one word."

"All right," said Benjamin. "But please understand. Naomi authorized you to investigate. But now you're instructing myself and others to potentially violate a legal agreement with a partner company. And to do it behind Nicola's back. Behind the back of the chief operating officer. We will. But are you certain you want Nicola out of the loop? I know there's always been a rivalry between the two of you, but—."

"Benjamin, this isn't personal. I have reason to question what is going on in this arrangement, and I have reason to question Nicola's involvement in it. And *we have no time.* I need to know *now.*"

Benjamin nodded. But he had a sense of deep foreboding. There was more to a company than numbers. Distrust could destroy a company inwardly.

Ah, well, he reflected. Fortune favors the bold.

"Your directive is understood," said Benjamin. "I will make it so. But I at least have to inform Naomi."

"All right," said Johanna.

"Is there anything else?" asked Benjamin.

"Yes. Talk to Noelle."

"Noelle?"

"Noelle Christien. Our contact person with the Distribution people. They handle both our chocolates and our shipping partner's materials. I know where our stuff goes. I want to know where their stuff goes too."

"Again, that may be a violation of confidentiality."

"Well, violate it! Ask her and find out!"

Benjamin laughed.

"Yes, Your Royal Majesty!"

Johanna hung up.

She put her iPhone away.

Johanna thought for a moment and then looked around. There, among a field of mostly female workers, was Jacob, slashing away, gathering pods. The ladies were infinitely amused. Barely a one had not slapped his posterior in passing, and broken into high giggles.

Jacob pretended to be irked. It was an act. He was eighteen, after all, and liked being the center of attention; and some of the girls there were not unattractive.

Johanna had put him there because she believed that to understand a company's operations, you had to actually engage in them. Enough, at least, to get a sense of what was going on. Enough to get people who *knew* what was going on to talk to you.

Her father had had that. That *total* empathy. He visited people in their homes when they were sick. Gave them presents when their children graduated from the schools that Chococoa helped pay for. Danced with them at Ghanaian holidays and celebrations. Wept with them when their parents died. He was loved. That love spilled over onto Johanna. It would spill over onto Jacob, if she could just keep him in the fields and out of Accra and its party houses and dance halls.

But there was no time. No time, *no time*.

And she hadn't been entirely honest with Benjamin. 'Big Pharma' wasn't the only odd thing going on. 'Freedom For The Children.' What was *that* all about? That had never made sense, not to Johanna. *Some* support for public relations purposes, fine. But Nicola's commitment of company funds and assistance was just plain crazy, over the top, *especially* now. Many of the things Nicola did seemed that way to Johanna, all show, no substance. But Chococoa was *hurting*, seriously, and Nicola had not cut back the company's charitable donations one jot.

It might have been a PR boost once, but now it was old news. It had nothing to do with the supply chain, the chain of production, and it made no sense.

It needed to be looked at, but Johanna wasn't in a position to do it. In a few minutes she's be back at her desk looking at Tama Harbor and their shipping operation courtesy of her laptop and Google Maps. She shook her head. Amazing how much supply chain information could be gathered online nowadays. The company security cameras alone let her actually see what was happening on the floor. That was exactly what she was going to spend the next few hours doing. It would make her coming visit to the Harbor go as smooth as silk. It might even make it unnecessary.

But there wasn't enough time for that *and* for visiting

one of Nicola's pet NGO's.

Maybe it was time to expose Jacob to Accra after all.

"Jacob!" she shouted.

He looked in her direction.

She waved him over.

He quit chopping at cocoa pods and walked over, stopping shortly midway to grit his teeth and do a little dance step of ninja moves, whipping his machete every which way.

"Goddamned mosquitoes," he swore, as he approached.

"Trying to circumcise the mosquitoes one by one with your machete," observed Johanna "isn't the most efficient solution. You could circumcise yourself that way, you know."

"How about just finding an insect repellent that *works?*" said Jacob. "Is *that* efficient?"

"The mosquitoes just want to get nuzzle your handsome posterior, Romeo," said Johanna, "like all the girls here."

"Yeah, well…" he mumbled, not sure what to say.

"It's time you took a break," said Johanna. "I want you to do something for me."

"What?" he said suspiciously.

"Go into town. Accra. I want you to visit one of the charities we're supporting. Freedom For The Children. Don't tell them who you are. Say you want to be a volunteer or something. Look around."

"Undercover work?"

"If thinking of it that way excites you."

"Undercover work in darkest Africa…"

"It's morning, idiot. The sun's out, and if you go now you'll be downtown by noon. Oh, and sorry: the clubs are closed in the daytime. Plus I want you back by late afternoon at the latest, understand?"

"Hey, who made you Hitler, *sis?*"

"Naomi. 'Johanna has top priority,' remember?"

Jacob still looked resentful. Johanna saw it, didn't

like it, and looked him in the eyes and put her hand on his shoulder.

"Look, Jacob. I'm sorry. Seriously, you've done a good job here. I know you want to see the town a little, and you really would be helping by stopping over at that Freedom place and giving me your report. Take a break. Have one of the managers send someone to drive you to town. Stop at a café. Go to a shop and get some fresh, decent clothes. Have a good lunch. Then go look around. Tell me what you see."

Jacob, surprised, hesitated for a moment.

"Johanna—"

"Yes?"

His eyes glanced left without his head moving. "OK, I'll go. Thanks! But there's something I'm seeing right now. I don't know, maybe I'm wrong—"

"What is it?"

"See that guy down there? Way to your left? Don't look directly. The man with the clipboard and the sunglasses?"

Jacob looked away. Johanna waited a second, and glanced left.

"I see him. Looks like one of the manager's assistants measuring operations. 'Knowing the supply chain means observing the supply chain,' remember? Thoughts of Chairman Johanna #345. Or he might be the government. They send inspectors out casually all the time."

"Yeah, well, this inspector's been watching you a whole lot."

Johanna shrugged. "You're not the only Anan with a cute posterior, baby brother."

"Maybe. But there's something about his build. His shoulders. He makes me think of someone."

"Who?"

"The guy who rammed into you on the motorcycle."

2

Nicola sat in the Board Room, alone. *Alone,* she thought. *Always alone.*

She shook the stray reflection off. *Sentiment. Useless.* She closed her eyes.

Slats of light coming through the blinds cut luminescent ribbons across the room and across Nicola herself. She sat there, spine erect, posture flawless, the tips of her fingers together. Calm, lovely, a portrait of Buddhist meditation.

Through her head ran various options, scenarios.

Was Kwaku the buyer? Was he finally moving to take complete control over the company? Unlikely. She knew that he was in fact operating non-criminal enterprises now, buying controlling shares, forming NGO's beyond Freedom For The Children. Expanding, always expanding. Emerging, partially and deceptively, into the public square. Into the light.

But why take formal control over something you controlled informally anyway? She had maintained an *illusion* of autonomy for Chococoa, but only because Kwaku had no greater interest in the firm, she assumed, than the money-laundering. The donations were no more than blackmail, payments to ensure that the Anans remained uninvolved and unharmed.

If the mystery buyer were some other entity entirely, Nicola might stay on as part of the purchase agreement, and Kwaku's influence might` persist through her. Or he could terrorize the new buyer and bring them to heel, as he had Nicola. Or Kwaku could just shrug his shoulders, and launder elsewhere. He owned multiple companies now, and companies collapsed. Would Chococoa's collapse really matter to him? Kwaku had alternative options. It might be an inconvenience, but nothing fundamental would change.

Unless Nicola changed it.

After her encounter with Kwaku nearly three years

earlier, Nicola soon began making plans, preparations, of her own. Kwaku was a problem, an obstacle. There were solutions to obstacles. Some simple, some radical.

Except that Kwaku had become a *complex* problem. An ethical problem. They had spoken a number of times after that first incident. He picked her brain, to *brand* himself, to apply her insights to his enterprises. Her skin crawled at the sound of his voice, his reptilian presence. It still did. But Kwaku was no simple thug. He had a vision and logic all his own. Nicola had not come to pity him—Kwaku had waded in too much blood for that. He derived his wealth from people's addictions and misery, and based his power on deliberate terror. He was a monster, pure and simple.

But under different circumstances he might not have been a monster. He was immensely intelligent, and ambitious, and he wanted to *do* something with that ambition, something beyond mere greed and terror. He had *consulted* with her, sought to learn from her. They had talked about appearance and reality, efficiency and operations, good and evil. Once he quoted Goethe: "I am part of that power which eternally wills evil and eternally works good," and in fact he *had* done good, decimating child traffickers, building schools, eliminating government corruption by shooting the corrupt—the corrupt that he disdained or that served him poorly or otherwise got in his way.

Just as he had worked his way like a tapeworm into Chococoa, so she too had slowly begun to get a sense of the fuller scope of Kwaku's activities and operations, and the more she learned, the more ambiguous they became. Kwaku realized that evil required good. Or at least many of the things associated with good, like competence, efficiency, order, predictability, profit, public relations, *perceptions*. His underground activities were now complimented by businesses and charities operating in the light of day. Honest profit fed into dishonest, and vice versa. Brutal exploitation worked in sync with a rough extralegal justice all his own.

Why? Kwaku wanted to pull strings behind the scenes. Strings in Accra, in Ghana, in Africa, in Europe. What was he after? After all this time she still didn't know.

But she did know that he kept *picking her brain*, he kept trying to involve her ever more deeply, incriminating her by informing her of activities she could never confess, because confessing them meant her extermination.

There were lines. Lines which she would not allow Kwaku to cross. The Anan family were not to be harmed, nor involved. She owed that much to Michael. Kwaku was not to *touch* them. Nor her. Not a *finger*. Chococoa might facilitate the movement of his criminal profits, but it was not to engage in the execution of his criminal activities.

He agreed to everything with a smirk, coddling her, *patronizing* her, giving in to her 'ethical' demands all the while making it clear that he could do anything he pleased, to anyone he pleased, any time at all.

Kwaku seemed to think that all companies, all nonprofits, all governments were as lawless and venal and criminal as himself, but that he, Kwaku, by *embracing* the nihilism they concealed even from themselves could deploy it more efficiently than these others, hobbled as they were with nonsense about serving the people, the public.

Kwaku sneered at such sentimentality. You could serve the public best by killing the right people, and you could make things work better and more equitably by killing a good many politicians, criminals and corporate profiteers.

It all came down to the logic of competition. Other criminals, in government or out, were his competitors. Erasing them from existence or putting them under his heel left Kwaku's organization all that much stronger. The *reduction* in crime, in corruption, in chaos, the social *uplift* that resulted, was just a happy incidental outcome.

Nihilism too was an idealism.

His paradoxes tempted her. *He* tempted her. He claimed that Ghana was better, that Chococoa was stronger, because of his winnowing efforts. Was he not right?

Nicola shook her head. No; no, it was all manipulation. Mind games. Cat and mouse. Sooner or later she had to end it. She *would* end it.

The door opened. Benjamin Anan walked in.

Nicola opened her eyes and looked at him. There was a moment of surprised silence.

"Nicola!" said Benjamin. "Why, hello. I—uh—wasn't expecting you."

She nodded.

"May I help you, Benjamin?"

"Um—" He hesitated. He'd entered the boardroom to access some of the legal hard copies of the firm's building blueprints, which were stored in the recessed cabinets. He wanted to see if the layouts of the R&D and Pharma sections matched the ostensible digital layout accessible on their intranet. As an attorney he'd read about, and even occasionally come across, hidden niches, false fronts, discrepancies. It was worth checking.

"I—I just thought I'd go over a few legal files. Business-related. You know." He laughed.

She looked at him without expression.

He had always been terribly intimidated by Nicola. Benjamin had an eye for the ladies, and ladies had always found Benjamin charming and had reciprocated. But Nicola was of an entirely different order of being. Each time he looked at her he felt like a ten-year old being introduced to a starlet, if not the Queen Mother. His normal eloquence deserted him. She had never connected with Benjamin as one human being to another. She had never connected with anyone there, really, other than Michael Anan.

Yet, somehow, unexpectedly, a strange sincerity welled up in him at that moment, and overflowed. That cool distance in her expression as she sat in her Director's chair… her almost plaintive sense of separateness, of isolation…

"Nicola," he said, "what *happened?*"

"What do you mean? To the company?"

"To *you.*"

"I don't understand what you mean."

"The firm. All we've done. Everything may fall apart. Don't you *care?*"

Her expression was glacial, her body motionless.

"Very much," she said.

"Then why are you just *sitting* there? It's as though the company has been frozen these past three years. You're—you're sitting there staring into space. Why aren't you *doing* something? Why aren't you—"

"If you want to see someone *emote*, Benjamin, I suggest you go to the Royal Shakespeare Theatre. I have work to do, maintaining operations and salvaging the future of this company, if possible, or overseeing its graceful transference to new hands if not. If you have something relevant to those ends, please share. If not, please leave."

Benjamin opened his mouth, but he could add nothing. Her eyes flashed. She dazzled. His usual abashed reaction returned, and choked him. He mumbled something, entirely forgot the blueprints for the moment, and turned and left.

Nicola was alone. She placed her fingertips against one another once more.

3

Benjamin stepped outside the boardroom. He took several steps down the corridor, stopped, and leaned against the wall.

Distrust could destroy a company, he had reflected.

Yes, he had thought, it could.

But if the company were falling apart already, what difference did it make?

He took out his smartphone and placed a call.

"Derek Eckland speaking."

Derek Eckland had been introduced to Benjamin by an older solicitor. The man considered him the finest private investigator in the London area specializing in the area of business. Eckland held a degree in computer science, had worked for the SAS, and was said to have contacts throughout the police and intelligence community.

If there was something to be found, Eckland would find it.

"Benjamin Anan here, Mr. Eckland."

"Ah, Mr. Anan. Good to hear from you. Is this a social call?"

"No," said Benjamin. "I want you to investigate someone."

"Name?"

"Nicola Cavalcanti."

"The head of your company?" said Eckland. "Interesting. Could you elaborate?"

"I am not planning a boardroom coup, Mr. Eckland. Nor am I looking for personal material with which to pressure anyone."

"I know. I don't do blackmail, Mr. Anan. You don't either. That's one of the reasons I like to work with you."

"What I do want to know is if there is any pressure *being* applied. We've been doing an analysis of our company, and while there don't appear to be any major financial sinks or obvious malfeasance, there have been a few decisions at the top level that—don't make sense. I'd like to know if Nicola's finances are being… augmented. Or drained."

"You want a breakdown of her finances?"

"I don't want to impinge on her privacy…"

"Impinging on privacy is what I do, Mr. Anan."

"I want an overview. An assessment. If something is

wrong, or odd, or questionable, I want you to point it out. Nicola is a key element in a situation the company is currently facing, and she is a blank. A mystery. She is an extremely private person, and I don't want to violate that privacy. But I want the mystery clarified."

"I will get right on it."

"How long will it take?"

"For an overview? Three days. A deep dive is a whole other story."

"Call me when your assessment is ready."

4

Once Jacob had gone to get ready for his visit to Accra, Johanna waited a moment, and then walked over one by one to the girls cutting cocoa pods off the trees.

Johanna smiled. She laughed. She nodded her head subtly back at the figure with the clipboard and the sunglasses in the distance, and said, "That man is following me."

As she walked on, the figure quietly followed along in her wake, making little notes.

And one by one, the girls and their machetes followed along in *his* wake.

And after a few more minutes of strolling along, Johanna came to a halt in a clearing. A slow cool breeze wafted through the palms; their wavering shadows danced along the grass; the mosquitoes murmured their soft background buzz; nature seemed calm and at peace. And Johanna turned and faced the man directly.

And a ring of women, lifting their machetes, closed in around him.

He turned to run.

They closed in tighter.

Dozens upon dozens of them.

He turned back to Johanna.

As she approached, one of the women tossed a

machete to her. Johanna caught the handle in the air and swung the machete in wide ugly circles as she got closer to the man in the sunglasses.

When she got close enough, she swung it at his head hard and stopped it at his jugular.

He dropped his clipboard.

The women crowded around them, machetes held high.

"Who the *hell* are you," hissed Johanna through grit teeth, "and why are you following me?"

The man raised his hands.

Slowly, delicately, using one thumb and one finger, he reached into his shirt pocket and took out a slim billfold and dropped it open.

Johanna snapped it out of his fingers with her free hand.

She held it up, comparing the face on the ID with that of the man.

The ID read: Joshua Mbebe Duvalier.

Interpol.

Chapter Seven

Big Pharma

1

"Oh, Benjamin," said Naomi. "I don't know."

Benjamin nodded. He understood her hesitation. But he was not a successful attorney for nothing. Ultimately the boundaries of a situation revealed itself. Some things were possible, some were not, and some actions needed to be taken, whether you liked them or not.

Unlike Johanna, however, he also understood the need for finesse. Honesty, of course, but presented with a certain rhetorical tact.

"I take it you have no objection to our investigating the R&D section."

"*Our* section, no. But the section we share with the partnering company? Yes, I do have concerns. You're the attorney, Benjamin. My understanding is that technically we lease the property to 'Big Pharma.' —Good grief, do they really call themselves that?"

"Absurdly, they do, and yes, the area is technically under lease."

"Technically? What does that mean exactly. We can't simply barge in."

"I mean technically and legally. There is a proviso in our agreement whereby Chococoa may investigate their designated space if we have reason to believe it may constitute a reasonable danger or 'ecological threat' to our personnel or the remainder of our facilities. I've drawn up a document to that effect which we can present."

"And do we any such reason?"

"Do *we* have any such reason to think so? No. But Johanna must. She is adamant that we investigate."

"*Curiosity* isn't enough."

Benjamin hesitated. Johanna could be curt, but this was not simple abruptness. Her tone had been unmistakable. This was mandatory. She hadn't been forthcoming concerning her reason, and Benjamin had his suspicions as to why.

She's trying to protect us. If there's nothing and we all look like idiots and get sued, we can put it all on her shoulders. Legally she is operating as a consultant to the company. I can place a firewall between her and Chococoa if necessary. We can separate the responsibility, and lighten any legal blowback. But obviously she doesn't think that will happen. Because... why?

"Johanna says she *must* know what's going on in R&D and in the Pharma installation. She sounds as though what she expects to find is significant. I can justify the inspection legally. Granted, there may be a legal battle if Big Pharma wishes to contend."

"And we have to go behind Nicola's back to do all this?"

"Again—plausible deniability. We can tell Nicola we did it to protect her."

"Which is a lie, I take it."

Benjamin spread his hands.

"I've looked at the paper trail. Apparently Chris approached Nicola with the news that a company based in Ghana called 'Big Pharma' wanted to partner with us. Apparently they harvest plants, nuts, minerals and other whatnot for eventual medicinal use, some of which they process here, some elsewhere in the EU. Marketing and public relations aside, Nicola delegates, as you know. It seemed a financial arrangement, not marketing, so she left it in Chris's hands. The two firms agreed to share the cost of shipping, which did in fact result in some savings for Chococoa. And we had some space assigned for future R&D development that was being unused. After Johanna left, Nicola cut the R&D budget to the bone and re-directed the funds to PR and increased charitable contributions. Big Pharma said that they wanted to use the space to treat their material in some fashion prior to sending it on. Since Chococoa products are distributed through Europe, and their treated materials are too, eventually they piggybacked on our distribution partners as well. Fees were agreed upon, Chris approved, Nicola signed off."

"It all seems above board."

"Except that their security criteria precludes our examination of their workspace. And their finished products. We don't know what they're doing. Or producing."

"Why do we *care* what they're doing?" said Naomi. "They're not a significant contributor to our cash flow. They're an incidental part, at best, of our supply chain. They've had no accidents, violated no rules, paid their fees in a timely fashion, they don't impinge on other operations. All they ask of us, not unreasonably, are secure facilities. How would *we* feel if we partnered with Hershey's or Godiva on shipping, and they broke into our work floor?"

Since Michael's stroke, Naomi had concentrated on care-giving. She had passed active management of the firm to Nicola and the family and management staff, and they all tended to assume that Naomi was unfamiliar with the business and its processes. Benjamin realized they were wrong.

Ultimately, however, he could not answer her.

"Johanna says do it," he said, simply.

"We're in financial difficulties, Benjamin. Now is not the time to risk lawsuits, and alienate business partners— or to go behind Nicola's back. Were you planning on going behind mine as well?"

"Naomi. No, of course not. Why else would I be here?"

"Johanna is *investigating*. Nicola remains in the leadership role. Johanna will need to clarify if she's going to take actions like these. Otherwise—I'm sorry."

2

Security pushed Sgt. Joshua Mbebe Duvalier into the chair inside Johanna's temporary quarters. They did not do so gently.

Outside a number of machete-wielding women were shouting and wailing.

The second security officer, the one who had patted Duvalier down, handed the contents of the man's pockets—a handkerchief, keys, a dedicated smartphone and a second billfold—to Johanna. She looked through the billfold, and her eyebrow arched as a driver's license with a name other than Duvalier appeared. The face—a strong, handsome face—was the same on both IDs. She scanned through the numbers on the smartphone. Not much of Ghana there; various European area codes for the most part.

She handed them back to the security guard, and crossed her arms.

"Talk," she said.

"I'll need to make a call," said the man. "For authorization."

"To your crime boss?" said Johanna. "Your driver's license is fake. Or is it your Interpol ID that's fake? Or both. I don't know, and you're not calling anyone. Why don't we go to the police station if you want to place a call? Or better yet, a newspaper office? They could take a clear picture of you to put on the front page. *Interpol Spies On Ghana Firm.* Sounds like a story to me."

The man said nothing.

"Better yet. You want authorization? I'll have some of the girls outside take a few snapshots of your face and your documents and upload them to the net on their smartphones. We can video this talk, and upload the video to YouTube as we're driving over to the police. That way you can be a media star by the time you arrive."

The man frowned.

"Talk," she said again.

He sighed. "I do have *some* discretion, I suppose."

Johanna detected an accent blurred by travel. Italian?

"I am so happy for you," she said. "Talk."

He shrugged. "What do you want to know?"

"Why did you smash into me on that motorcycle?"

Now *his* eyebrow rose.

"I don't know what you're talking about. I don't even drive a motorcycle."

"My brother said you reminded him of a man who tried to drive into me the other day."

"Maybe we have the same build. Or maybe your brother is just a little paranoid. Was the man wearing a face helmet?"

Johanna nodded.

The man jerked his chin at the billfold in the guard's hand. "That's a car license in your hand. Not a motorcycle license."

"That proves nothing."

"It proves nothing either way. Sorry you almost had an accident, but it wasn't me."

Johanna pursed her lips.

"You say you're with Interpol?"

"That's right."

"Why should I believe you?"

"Call my office! I'm not involved in deep cover, just investigating. Go to the Interpol web site and type in my name and go to my agent's page!"

"What are you investigating?"

He looked at the security guards. "May we speak privately?"

Johanna held out her hand. The nearest guard took his pistol out and put it in her hand. She gave a nod of her chin, and everyone left.

She pulled a chair over and, gun in hand, sat facing her guest.

"We're speaking privately," she said.

"Interpol is investigating Big Pharma."

"Big pharma in general? Why bother us?"

"Big Pharma is the name of the company with which your firm has a shipping agreement."

"You're joking."

"They change their name frequently. It was re-registered about two weeks ago."

Marketing people, thought Johanna. She needed to update the model simulation. God, how easy it was to get out of touch with developments. Information flow deserved a supply chain analysis all of its own. She would have to make a note.

But that wasn't the main thing. *I was right. They're dealing drugs,* she thought.

But she wanted it to come from Mr. Interpol as a shocking revelation. It wouldn't do to let the authorities think that Chococoa had had its suspicions about the subject without first contacting them.

"So why aren't you investigating 'Big Pharma'? Why bother us?"

"First, because they store the materials that they ship with you, here. We want to take a quiet look at it. But the moment you got here, you started going over everything. Their security has heightened."

"Why do you want to take a look at their materials?"

"We believe it to be contraband."

"No!" said Johanna. "You mean like—drugs?"

He frowned and nodded. "Very likely."

"I can't believe it!" said Johanna.

"Believe it," growled the man.

He really was very good looking, thought Johanna.

She calculated. The firm shared some shipping costs with Chococoa, and it paid for rental space at the home facility. Every cent counted at this point, but Big Pharma's cash flow contribution was not so large that Chococoa would rise or fall based on their association. On the other hand, if Chococoa personnel were involved in drug trafficking, the corruption might well involve embezzlement. It could be a relevant factor—possibly even a major one—in the company crisis.

But who in the company could have facilitated it? She couldn't imagine that Nicola was involved. Drug trafficking was poor public relations. For Nicola that would be like breaking all Ten Commandments at once. For once, Johanna agreed: at this point in time, Chococoa could not afford bad press. Not at all.

Yet somewhere here was an opportunity. Could full cooperation with the authorities gain Chococoa a *quid pro quo* of some sort? What sort? Johanna didn't yet know. But she did know this was a development with potential.

She calculated. And re-calculated.

"Miss Anan. We'd like to take a look at their materials. Can you assist us? It's a simple question."

"Legally, Mr. Interpol, I don't believe we can. We have a signed agreement with these people."

"And you would never violate that agreement."

"Never."

"You would never look the other way."

"Never. If it got into the news, Mr. Interpol—"

"We can keep it entirely out of the news."

"And it—it just puts our company at such *risk*—"

"If you could simply look the other way, Miss Anan, the authorities would be grateful. Very grateful."

"Ah, well, *gratitude*, gratitude is a wonderful thing, but you really can't take gratitude to the bank, can you,

Mr. Interpol?"

"The authorities would owe you a favor."

"A *big* favor," said Johanna.

"A favor."

"A *major* favor," said Johanna.

He rolled his eyes.

"Don't push your luck, Miss Anan. A favor."

"Starting with a full report on what you find."

"A full *unofficial* report? Verbally? Sure."

Now Johanna took a moment to consider. But only because it was part of the dance.

"We have a deal," she said.

3

"*Oui?*"

"Am I speaking to Noelle Christien?"

"You are."

"I am Benjamin Anan, the principal solicitor for Chococoa, Ltd."

"Ah, Mr. Anan, how do you do? I've met a number of your associates. They speak very well of you."

"They speak very well of *you*, Ms. Christien. It's a pleasure to make your acquaintance at long last."

"How may I help you, Mr. Anan?"

"Well—it's rather a sensitive issue, Ms. Christien. You see…"

"Excuse me, Mr. Anan, but are you near a laptop, by any chance?"

"Yes, as a matter of fact."

"Could you possibly Skype me? I'm afraid you called as I was sending some material off online, and immediate delivery is absolutely critical. I can speak and type on my laptop well enough, but less so on two separate devices."

"Of course. One moment."

Benjamin took his laptop out of his briefcase, opened it up, and was online in under a minute. He put a Skype call through to Noelle Christien of Coeur De Lion Distributors & Partners S.A.

He waited a moment and suddenly Noelle Christien's mellifluous voice came through.

"Mr. Anan?"

"I hear you, Ms. Christien. I'm afraid I don't see you."

She sighed. It was quite a charming sound. Benjamin had a weakness for French women. More accurately, he had a weakness for all women exhibiting a pulse. But *French* women with pulses, ah, they were a cut above. There was something about the lilting accent he found ravishingly charming, bird-like, and Ms. Christien deployed hers with unusual elegance. It was slightly off in some indefinable way that lingered with him, like a thorn. But it was a lovely thorn, the sort of voice he would enjoy hearing recite actuarial statistics, and it lifted him from his recent gloom. Alas, bitter experience taught him that this meant that she was probably an octogenarian with one eye. But he could daydream, and her voice was nothing if not an invitation to do so.

"*Alors*," she said, "video, no video. *Pah.* Let us proceed. You are too busy to wait as I fiddle, I am sure."

"Indeed," he said.

"And so?"

"Our company is doing a supply chain analysis from top to bottom. As you know, Coeur De Lion takes the finished chocolate products produced at our factory and distributes them to vendors and locations throughout Europe and North America."

"For the most part. I understand that you have people of your own distributing your products to stores and cafes in Derby itself and the immediate surrounding areas."

"Yes," said Benjamin. "And there is a subsidiary firm handling distribution outside Europe, but I understand that it too is a subdivision of Coeur De Lion."

"For legal purposes, yes."

"We understand you also distribute the output of a

company with whom we partner—'Big Pharma'?"

"Yes." She giggled a charming trill. "*Pardon.* That name! Well, the previous one was worse. That company changes names like children change bandages on their fingers. Yes, we take what they produce at your Derby plant, and distribute the items to various European locations."

"May I ask to whom?"

"You may *ask*, Mr. Benjamin, but I am not sure I am authorized to say. I would need to pass along your request, and confirm permission with the appropriate contacts of that company."

"Is the information confidential?"

"Even that information is confidential."

"May I ask if I may *reasonably assume* that you try to deliver our products and theirs together to the same locations, when the end delivery locales are the same? That would seem to be the efficient thing to do."

"You may assume whatever you like, reasonably or otherwise."

"I see."

"*Je suis désolé,* Mr. Anan. We must protect our confidences."

"I quite understand. It's the proper thing to do. However—"

"*Oui?*"

"Unofficially, Ms. Christien—privately, just between the two of us—our two companies may or may not be experiencing a bit of a falling out tomorrow. There may be a bit of turbulence in other respects too. Do please keep this to yourself. Coeur De Lion has always handled Chococoa well; we don't want you to be caught by surprise. Or to expect surprises—it's equally possible it may all come to nothing. But there are things that..."

There was a momentary silence. Suddenly the screen flickered and there was the face of Noelle Christien of Coeur De Lion Distributors & Partners S.A.

Benjamin all but gasped.

"Mr. Anan. Can you see me now? I can see you."

She was a slim and willowy brunette, thirtyish, with *freckles*, of all things, and grey eyes, and a waterfall of thick hair, and Benjamin could feel his heart throbbing in his chest.

Benjamin regarded himself as a connoisseur of female beauty. He realized that everything about Ms. Christien's features were *technically* wrong—her eyes were just a little too big, and her nose just a bit too aquiline, and her lips just a bit too red, and her neck just a bit too long. Yet when you mixed all the elements together, Benjamin simply melted. He gaped like a ten-year-old.

"Mr. Benjamin?"

He coughed. Repeatedly. "Yes. Um. Yes!"

"You can see me, Mr. Benjamin?"

"Oh, yes, indeed!"

"Mr. Benjamin, our companies have had a long and mutually beneficial relationship. If things are entering a period of transition, and we can assist in any fashion, please feel free to call on me."

"Oh I will!"

"Is there any way I can help?" she said.

Bear my children! sprang to his mind, but not his lips.

"Yes… well… perhaps we should schedule a meeting. In person. Yes, we should. We really must. We must. We can discuss… things! Yes. Yes, things!"

Ms. Christien gave him a somewhat bemused look. He suspected that she had divined some tiny iota of the asteroid-level impact she had had on him. He swore right there that even if Chococoa and Big Pharma and the EU and Global Capitalism Itself sputtered out and imploded over the next few months, he and Ms. Christien would be having a dinner together in the near future. A dinner to remember.

But he was also an honorable person, and he meant what he said. Coeur De Lion had served them well, and they would not be serving Coeur De Lion well if they kept their distribution partner in the dark about Big Pharma's mysterious secretiveness and about Chococoa's possible demise.

He cleared his throat.

"There are things you should be aware of, Ms. Christien, and we should discuss them. Not over Skype, however. Will you be in the Derby area or thereabouts in the near future, by any chance?"

"I shall be in London in two days time, Mr. Benjamin. I could easily stop over at your London offices. Or even catch an East Midlands train and visit your Derby plant, if you wish."

Two days! His heart beat even harder.

"Golly, that would be *wonderful*, Ms. Christien." (Had he really said *golly*? In his mind, he kicked himself savagely.)

"Call me Noelle, please," she said in that lovely, lingering, voice.

"Call me Benjamin, Ms. Chri—Noelle."

They both laughed simultaneously, for a reason neither could name, and they both hesitated to log off and end the call, and again neither could quite say why.

After running through several more variations of "Goodbye," Benjamin reluctantly ended the call.

The moment he did, it rang.

Noelle again! thought Benjamin, picking up instantaneously.

It was Johanna.

"Johanna. I have wonderful news!" he said, about to babble about Noelle Christien. He caught himself, and sobered up. "No, sorry, I have terrible news. I have bad news. Awful news. Naomi refuses to allow—"

"Forget Naomi. We need to coordinate."

He sighed.

"I'm trying to *tell* you something, Jo. *Listen!* Naomi feels we simply don't have enough cause to break into the Big Pharma operations here. She says that—"

Johanna laughed.

"Is *Interpol* enough cause?" she said.

"What?"

"Tell Naomi that Interpol is about to launch a raid on Big Pharma here."

"A *raid*? Here? You mean here as in 'on Chococoa facilities in Ghana'?"

"Yes, in Ghana, and not exactly on Chococoa, just the warehouse, and no, not a *raid* raid. I mean, not with guns blazing. Let's just say a little information-gathering venture. With our unofficial assistance. We're trying to keep it quiet, too. But word gets out—it always does. That's why we have to get into their operation at Derby *now*, in a coordinated fashion. If Big Pharma sees something happening in Ghana, they're likely to clean up whatever's going on at the main plant in Derby."

"*Interpol* is going in, you say. Is that correct?"

Johanna nodded vigorously, forgetting that Benjamin could not see her.

"They have a man here who's been casing our joint operation," she said. "He seems to have convinced himself that Big Pharma and Chococoa are running on separate tracks."

"As they are."

"As they are. And it's good that Interpol thinks so. But he wants a close look at what Pharma is shipping. Our cooperation should ensure that we get a clean bill of health. He wants to move quickly."

"How quickly?"

"Two hours from now."

"Two *hours*?"

"Two hours. His cover was blown. Our people in the fields know a man from Interpol is here. You know how word spreads in the fields. It won't be long until the Pharma people here find out. He can't wait."

"And you want *us* to move in at the same time too?"

"That's what coordination means, Ben. Can you do it? No—no, forget that. *Do it!*"

She hung up.

Benjamin looked at the phone.

He blinked a moment.

Then he called Naomi, the Cult of Jo, and Security.

4

Jacob looked at himself in the mirror. He wanted to whistle. *Looking good!*

The Ghanaian tailor thought so too. He actually clapped his hands in a round of applause.

"Very nice, young Mister. *Very* nice."

Hey, thought Jacob, *Johanna said to get a change of clothing. Right?* How was he supposed to walk into the offices of an international NGO like Freedom For The Children smelling of insect repellent and looking like the sweaty, mosquito-bitten teenager that he was?

Jacob had proposed various spy scenarios to himself as the driver took him to Accra. He would pretend to be a young Ghanaian looking for a job; he would pretend to be a young journalist. Spy movie bullshit! Best to forget all that, and just say, truthfully, that he was the family member of a major donor. All he had to do was show them his ID and the Anan name. That would do it. It was like politics. He'd watched *House Of Cards*; he knew how things worked. Wave money. Doors open.

And hey—Johanna said herself that he should get a change of clothing. Why not an elegant change? Chococoa would foot the bill.

And so Jacob found himself in the center of Accra at the tailor shop, dressed like John Travolta in *Saturday Night Fever*, in fine shoes, a blindingly white vest and suit that would reflect away the hot sun. *Nice!*

Admiring himself in the tailor's mirror, he pointed a finger straight up, Travolta-like, and did a dance twirl and laughed.

The tailor held up his ancient oaken finger. "One last item, young sir! He carefully knotted a cobalt-blue business tie around Jacob's neck, straightened it, smoothed the collar, and stepped back.

Jacob looked in the mirror, and was surprised to see his image suddenly look ten years older, transformed into the very model of a successful young entrepreneur on the cover of *GQ*.

He had never really seen himself as an entrepreneur before. His posture straightened. He liked what he saw.

Jacob gave the tailor's assistant the information needed to put the purchase on the Chococoa expense account, signed, and stepped out into the bustling Accra streets.

Appreciative glances from passing girls and ladies were not slow in coming. Men too noted the expense and cut of his clothing—despite his age, this was a person of some stature. It supercharged him. He was free of the mosquitoes, the sweat, free of his dopey big-mouthed sister. He was on the town—ecstatic.

Suddenly, and for the first time, he loved Ghana. Seeing it glittering below him like a jewel as their helicopter rose above the city had impressed him. But now, moving along with the crowd, swimming among the people, *his* people, like a fish in a vast pulsing school, he felt exalted. Yes, *his* people. And they were a beautiful, dynamic people; women with long elegant traditional dresses and jewelry and headdresses, alongside other women with cut-off denim jeans and reggae Bob Marley T-shirts, alongside manly laborers and striding dynamic men in business suits and portfolios talking into iPhones. *Afrobeats*, a unique hybrid of highlife and hip-hop music filled the street corners. The men had strong, focused, intrepid faces, they had *style*, they walked with a confidence and intensity that seeped into Jacob as he walked beside them. Strangely, he felt himself growing into manhood. The noise, the crowds, the energy, the bustle. These were a people with a future. And he was one of them.

He laughed. After he was done with the Freedom people, he would hit every dance floor and cafe with a pretty girl in it that he passed!

But right now he was on a mission for the company. He squared his shoulders and, still smiling, moved forward with determination. He would get the job done.

He was a man. *A Ghanaian!*

5

Johanna put her arm in the arm of Sgt. Joshua Mbebe Duvalier and announced their engagement.

The ring of girls surrounding them exploded in cheers and whistles. Machetes waved in the air. More girls, and boys, and men and women, and then what seemed like everything in Ghana that had two legs and a few that had four all ran towards Johanna and Duvalier, shouting and cheering.

"We're going to be *married!*" she shouted, and planted an immense kiss on Duvalier's horrified face. "Work time over. *Party time!*"

The roar of the crowd tripled and quadrupled. Spontaneous dancing broke out. Bottles appeared. Boom boxes popped from lockers and duffel bags and Sarkodie's Afrobeats music started thundering. The fields began writhing with people the way the trees writhed with palms.

Johanna grabbed Duvalier's hand.

"*We* want to be *alone!*" she yelled in Akan, and as the crowd howled, "WoooOOOoooo!" she threaded grinning through the crowd with Duvalier, heading toward the Big Pharma storage area.

Someone thrust a bottle into her hand. She took it, and took another one too, and put it in Duvalier's.

"Are you out of your *mind?*" he yelled.

The rising tide of noise swallowed everything.

In a matter of minutes they arrived. Johanna threw open the door of the storage warehouse, and swept in, twirling and hooting and laughing. On one side of the plant a half dozen Chococoa maintenance people were moving sacks of cocoa beans. On the other, the Big Pharma area, two tight-mouthed guards stood next to several towers of sacks not far from a forklift.

"*Party Time!*" she shrieked, as the sounds of the revelers streamed in from behind her. She laughed drunkenly, and threw her bottle to the Big Pharma guards. "Drink up, *Chale!*"

The Chococoa people looked at each other, clapped their hands, and ran to the door and out into the crowd before the bottle even landed in their hands. The Big Pharma guard looked at the bottle, sitting in his hand, and then at the other guard.

"*Woo!*" cried Johanna, whirling around, spinning, falling to the floor and laughing drunkenly. The music streaming in past the door grew louder.

The guards looked at Duvalier, who stood there with a bottle of his own. He looked back at them, blinked a few times, belched as loudly as he could, then fell to his knees, and on his face.

The guards looked at one another.

Then they too went, "*Woo-ooo!*" and ran out to join the party.

Johanna jumped up instantly and shut and locked the door.

Duvalier stood up and shook his head.

"You are the *craziest*—"

"The guards are gone. The place is empty. No one can hear anything we do or say over the noise. Tomorrow the guards won't remember a thing. And if they *do* remember anything, they'll deny leaving their post. Come on, I even got you to put on your funky little James Bond backpack before I made the announcement. What more do you want?"

Duvalier grumbled regardless and he pulled his backpack off. *Engaged?* That could ruin his reputation.

He unzipped the side of the backpack and took out a thin scalpel, a probe, square plastic tabs that looked like pill boxes, and a thin device with a pulsing blue light that looked like a tricorder from *Star Trek*.

He moved toward the Big Pharma sacks smoothly and professionally, stuck the scalpel in this one, the probe in that one, removed tiny samples from one sack after another, and placed them quickly and carefully in separate slots in the pill box, sealing each one up with an interior cap. Every now and then he would take a sample and put it in the tricorder device and wait for a reading. A puzzled look began to appear on his face after several minutes, but he continued the process with surgical regularity.

Finally he stopped, put everything back in the backpack, and pulled out yet another instrument that simply looked weird. He pointed it at the towers or sacks and swept it up and down, like radar, turning and pointing it from various directions as it made snapshot-like sounds.

"What's that?" said Johanna.

"Portable dog."

"Excuse me?"

"Portable dog. You know how the Post Office brings in dogs to sniff out drugs in packages?"

Johanna nodded.

"This is a portable dog. In fact it's a portable super-dog. It can make out scents behind solid brick."

"Really."

"Yes."

He worked on, fast, efficiently, methodically.

Time passed.

Johanna scratched.

"So, Mr. Interpol," said Johanna, after a while. "*Are you engaged?*"

"No," he said, working with focused concentration.

"Are you married?"

"No," he said, continuing to work with focused concentration.

"Have you ever been married?"

"*No*," he said, *trying* to work with focused concentration.

"Do you ever think about getting married?"

"NO," he said, failing to work with focused concentration.

"Wow, I guess you must not like girls... you *do* like girls, don't you?..."

"Will you *shut up!*" he roared.

Johanna smiled.

She leaned against one of the Big Pharma sacks and began whistling "Love Is A Many-Splendored Thing," as Duvalier moaned in agony.

6

The offices of Freedom For The Children were on one of the higher floors of a skyscraper near the center of Accra. Jacob was surprised, and not pleasantly: he felt that donations for children were supposed to go to children, not high-ticket corporate rental. Was this where Chococoa's own donations were going? He'd have to make a note of it to Johanna and Nicola.

There were multiple security people at the door. They checked his paperwork and walked him thought a metal detector. The metal detector was a surprise. He asked about it. The guard said something about "politics," but without much elaboration, or interest. The guard asked about the purpose of Jacob's visit, his length of stay in Ghana, whether anyone would be joining him. The questions seemed more pointed than were necessary, and Jacob felt the guard noted the young man's youth and attire with a whiff of envy. Was he expected, said the guard? Yes, Jacob lied. He wanted it to be a surprise visit. You saw more that way. Even the reaction to a surprise visit might reveal something. The guard hesitated, perhaps thinking to call to confirm, but he looked at the quality cut of the suit and tie again. With a grunt, the guard pointed to the elevators.

Jacob located the floor on the corporate roster, took the elevator up, stepped out into an elegantly austere corridor. He walked to the end.

"Freedom For The Children" was written on the frosted glass pane of the door at the very end, along with versions in French and *Twi*.

Jacob opened the door.

It was a receptionist's office. It was empty. No one sat in the seats for visitors. No secretary was there to greet them. The lights were on. There was a phone on the desk. A computer. A filing cabinet. He looked around, and opened it. It was empty.

"Hello?" he said. "*Hello?*"

To his left was an adjoining door. Jacob went to it and knocked.

He knocked louder.

No one came. "*Hello?*"

He pushed at the door handle. Hard. It didn't open.

He noticed that the handle seemed old. Ghana in general was like that. Tribalism and technology cheek to jowl. Things from the 1950's, indeed from pre-history, seemed to casually exist side-by-side with things from the Apple Store and Nike, the old and the modern in a strange collage.

Jacob looked at the lock closely, and remembered an episode from one of the endless mystery shows that Benjamin was always watching and to which he dragged relatives unable to escape. In the episode, a tobacco-chewing American gumshoe had slipped out a credit card and worked the lock carefully with a sawing motion and it opened. Jacob looked around. Low-tech had its advantages: there were no security cameras that *he* could see.

What the hell. This trip was supposed to be an adventure.

He got out his plastic Student ID and slipped it in between the door and the jamb. It wasn't as easy as the movie made it look. Getting the card between the strike plate and against the curve of the latch was a chore. It took muscle to move it in deeper, and once he lost his grip and the ID slipped inside the door into the inner offices. *Damn!*

But he carried a plastic fitness center ID card too. He tried again, pressing against the latch carefully and assiduously, and—it opened!

Jacob slowly opened the door and quickly snatched up his fallen ID. He looked around the office space. It was empty. No desks, no computers, no phones, no people. Nothing. Empty space.

He walked around the floor. There was no notice of vacancy, nothing taped to a wall. The lights were on, though the blinds on the windows were all down. He took a few pictures of it on his iPhone and thought of sending it to Johanna, but what was there to send? Had it maybe just been a recent unannounced move? Strange that there was no notice on the door or office or anywhere else. And why leave the lights and the electricity on?

He turned to go. As he did, he noticed a digital recorder on the floor by the inside of the door, near an electric socket. He bent down and pressed the Play button. Nothing happened. Was the battery dead? He turned it around and looked to see if it might have an internal cord. He snapped open a compartment, and indeed it did. He pulled the cord out and plugged it in the wall, and pressed the Play button.

The sounds of a busy office soared out. Keyboards clacking, phones beeping, calls and conversations and coffee machines percolating. If he'd been sitting in the waiting room, the interior would have sounded like Microsoft.

He pressed the Off button and everything was silent and empty again.

Jacob stepped outside and shut the door behind him, making sure it was locked. He went through the receptionist's desk. There was nothing in the interior drawers. The computer was on, but had no history, no applications and no connection to the internet. The phone worked, but there was no record of calls or lists of contacts. The appointments book on the desk was empty.

These were the head offices of a globally active Ghana-based charity sending millions in donations to manage to Chococoa alone, and receiving six figures in donations from Chococoa for the privilege of providing the service. And there was nothing there!

But since there was nothing there, there was nothing more to do, he supposed.

He scratched his head, and left.

Jacob avoided the guard on the way out. There was something about the man he didn't trust. Maybe it was the fact that the man didn't seem to trust him. But that was a part of being in security, he supposed.

Whatever it was, once he'd left the skyscraper behind, Jacob felt the same rush of energy and freedom that he felt before when he hit the streets and joined the crowd.

He'd have to call Johanna and tell her about what he'd seen, of course. But if he did it right away, she'd say, "Get back here and harvest some more cocoa pods!" He had had enough of *that*. Time for seeing what the dance floors were like around here! And if it was maybe a little early for that, at least there was time to stop at a cafe and chat up a cute girl.

"Hey, you're a pretty boy," said a *dazzlingly* cute girl, slipping her arm into his. "Your papa a tailor or something?" She slid her hand over his white lapel and down along his waist as they walked along arm in arm. *Way* down along his waist. "I ain't seen nothin' packaged so nice not since Christmas."

Jacob tried to say hello but barely managed to gurgle. The girl's head was a wild burst of long dreadlocks down to her hips, her eyes were black pearls, the clothes she had on—well, the clothes she *almost* had on—were a combination of leather and spangles and Ghanaian necklaces that would have graced a pop star. Her ringed fingers slid up his lapel again. Jacob thought they would burn a hole through the material.

She looked to her right and there was an alley.

She looked at Jacob and smiled mischievously and leaned in and whispered in his ear. "Pretty boy, give me a kiss."

"*Sure!*" said Jacob.

With a high giggle she pulled him into the alley, and, pressing her body against his, gave Jacob a kiss that, if he were old enough to have fillings, would have melted them all, and set the metal popping and fizzing.

He looked at her, astonished and amazed, and tried to come up with something sophisticated to say other than "*Duhh...*," the only thing that came immediately to mind.

But instead Nature took over, and he grabbed her passionately, bending over her to kiss her as she laughed.

Ghana is Heaven on Earth!, he thought.

Then a bottle hit him on the back of his head, and there was darkness; and a thick dark hood was quickly pulled down over his face.

7

A thousand miles away, at about the same time, several people came together outside the entranceway door to the Research & Development facilities of the Chococoa factory at Derby in the United Kingdom.

Jack Sweeney arrived first; his two associates had their hands full with an unexpected mechanical breakdown in Sorting, and could not make it. Next a four-person factory vehicle drove up. In front were Popeye and Chococoa's beefy Chief of Security, Bill Shaw, who drove.

Behind them sat two of Popeye's guests—James J. Aschenblum, a retired industrial chemist formerly employed by European drug manufacturing firms, and consulting pharmaceutical operations manager R. Faisal

Singh. Occasional poker buddies, both owed Popeye a notable amount of money. Today's visit would diminish the amount. Somewhat.

Next Benjamin Anan arrived by foot, accompanied by a tall hulking security guard approximately as wide as he was tall.

Finally Naomi Anan arrived, and disembarked from an elegantly styled Citroen-like plant vehicle designed especially for her and Michael Anan.

Benjamin had notified her about Interpol and Big Pharma at the Ghana facility. The picture had changed.

Sweeney explained the situation with Sorting; Popeye explained that his guests would be looking for whatever they might spot, and report directly afterwards; Benjamin explained to the security people that the people in this part of the section would be Chococoa employees, but the personnel they were about to meet in the next section belonged to Big Pharma, not Chococoa, and might take offense at their freely wandering about.

Their official story was that concern had been expressed or leaked—never mind by whom—that materials or processes in the Big Pharma section posed a potential environmental hazard, and that they were allowed if not required by law to make a spot check in such eventualities.

"Are we ready, gentlemen," said Benjamin.

Everyone nodded.

The corridor entranceway was barred by a security guard even more mammoth than the mammoth figure accompanying Benjamin.

Benjamin approached the guard.

"Guard, please stand aside. We've here to undertake a brief review of the inner facilities."

"I'm sorry, sir," said the guard, "but my orders are not to allow anyone in without the direct prior approval of the Director of Finance alone."

"He is not available."

"Then I can't allow you or your party in, sir. I'm

sorry."

Benjamin stepped aside. Naomi Anan stepped up. The guard's eyes widened.

"Guard, do you know who I am?"

"Yes, Madame."

"You do realize that I am the acting owner of this firm, and your employer."

"Yes, Madame."

"Please step aside then, and let us pass."

He hesitated. "That would be against my direct orders, Madame."

The guard had spent twenty years in the military; old habits died hard.

Naomi looked surprised, and considered. "Guard, what is your name?"

"Philip P. Bull, Madame," he said.

"Mr. Bull, you're fired. Go away."

He blinked.

His massive frame relaxed. He removed his cap from his unexpectedly bald head, scratched an ear, and sighed.

"Yes, Madame," he said.

His mouth eased into a wistful smile. *Well, such is life!* it seemed to say.

"But show up in Personnel first thing tomorrow," said Naomi. "We're going to need a new guard for this area, and you seem singularly qualified. Enjoy your evening."

"*Yes,* Madame!" said the guard, instantly at attention again. He looked around with a bemused expression, as though he'd won a small but welcome amount on the lottery, and walked jauntily off.

"Gentlemen," said Naomi, adding, almost in a tone of warning, "*and* Benjamin—you may proceed."

The driver of her vehicle opened her door. She seated herself, and headed back to Michael's side, reflecting that she would probably be reading an Ian Fleming to him tonight.

"Gentlemen," said Benjamin, as he indicated the doorway entrance.

They walked down a long wide grim corridor, their footsteps echoing spookily. To the left was the door to the firm's R&D laboratory; at the end was the door to Big Pharma.

"Let's start with our own division," said Benjamin, stopping by the R&D door. He put his hand on the knob.

"Let me go in first," said Sweeney. "I believe I know a few of the people inside."

Sweeney entered.

A ripple of surprise and attention radiated through the men and women in R&D as he walked in. *No* one just walked into the R&D section nowadays. And several more new faces followed in behind him! The looks the people inside gave each other announced that the arrival of Benjamin's crew was so unusual that no one quite knew what to do.

So, apparently, they decided not to do anything.

Everyone shrugged, and got back to work.

Benjamin, who had never seen the R&D department was neither impressed not unimpressed. In most respects it was like a tiny scaled-back replica of the outer work floor, mixed up with a university chemistry lab. Various machines he didn't understand twirled like cheerleaders spinning batons. People in white coats walked about, peered at tubes, and made notes on clipboards. Benjamin looked and felt a bit like over-dressed partygoers who had accidentally stumbled into a medical school with massively oversized air conditioning units.

"Eddie! Hey!" said Sweeney, waving at a man adjusting an instrument that looked like a microscope. "Hey—Shankar! What, they haven't fired you yet?" he called.

Eddie lifted a hand and indicated he was still working on his instrument. Shankar, a Pakistani, walked over with a big grin.

"Jack Sweeney? You weasel! What are you doing here? This place is only for people who know arithmetic!"

"Just thought I'd say hi. Brought some friends."

Sweeney jerked a thumb at the group milling behind him. "Guests of the company. They asked for a tour, and the people upstairs said OK."

"Well—welcome, everyone. Some of the things we work on here are proprietary. 'Secret formulas' and all that, so we discourage casual walk-ins. I'm afraid we don't have very many visitors. But if Sweeney says you're approved, I suppose you are."

Shankar pointed to the far end of the room. "There's a cafeteria at the far end with vending machines and tables and coffee. There's a sink there too. Also medical gloves and face masks. I recommend you put them on if you're going to poke around all over. There's nothing particularly toxic on the main floor here, but you see that unit over there?"

The group's eyes all turned in the direction of what looked like a modernist greenhouse set in the center of the room. There were a variety of plants and seeds throughout, even a full-scale cocoa tree. At the same time there were sealed-off areas within the greenhouse that looked even more medically high-tech, like alien eruptions from NASA.

"Some of the items in *there* are toxic, which is why they're sealed off. And some of the plants and hybrids are being grown in specially designed sealed environments. We'd rather not have you walk in if any of you have a head cold or something infectious."

"And don't help yourself to any chocolate samples," said a small, rotund man who had just walked up, bearing a spotty face underneath his florid red hair and thick eyeglasses. He patted his considerable belly. "They may be experimental, and you may regret taking a bite. Bob Ellingham here," he said, offering his hand around to shake. "Unit Manager. How can I help you gentlemen?"

"We just wondered if you could give us a tour," said Benjamin.

"Certainly," said Ellingham. "Just watch you don't get in the way."

"I may stop and chat a bit with Ed and Shankar here. We used to work on the floor together outside till they moved on up."

"No problem," said Ellingham.

"I'd love to see that greenhouse-like installation," said Aschenblum to the Unit Manager. "You seem to have some fairly advanced equipment in there."

"Eric," called Ellingham to a youngish-looking blond fellow. "Get this guy a face mask and take him around the lab area, would you?"

Aschenblum and Eric strolled off in the direction of the greenery. Popeye and Singh drifted off too, inspecting the larger machinery, leaning their heads together for a whisper now and again. Shaw, Chocococa's Chief of Security, peppered Ellingham with questions, distracting him as all concerned snooped. Benjamin, feeling rather useless, stood around for a moment and then headed to the cafeteria for a wretched vending machine Earl Grey. He checked his email. He tried to find pictures of Noelle Christien on Google Images to pine over.

Slowly, after twenty minutes or so, the invaders straggled in.

"Well?" said Benjamin, popping the phone shut. "Anything worth noting?"

Popeye opened his mouth, but shut it again, deferring to his guests with a hand gesture.

Singh, the operations consultant, said, "This is an entirely functional, conventional, not particularly unimpressive research operation. I can't go into specifics, since the new blends of chocolates that they're trying to develop are proprietary formulas that I have not studied. But it all seems—well, the best thing I can say is bland. About what you'd see in any small under-funded R&D operation in chocolate anywhere."

"I thought significant funds were being funneled to R&D," said Benjamin.

"They must be being funneled to waste disposal." He waved his hand. "The equipment here—everything—it needs updating. Badly. There's just not much else to say. Mr. Aschenblum?"

Aschenblum nodded. He looked at Benjamin. "If you'll forgive me, Mr. Anan—I was under the impression that you were looking for something, shall we say, exotic? I'm often called in when plant or pharmaceutical businesses suspect employees of—*creative* uses of their supplies and equipment for private use or sales."

"And you found—?"

"Nothing. There is nothing of the sort going on here."

"Everything is legitimate?"

"Everything is *dull*. But, legitimate? Yes."

"Far as the eye can see," added Popeye. "You concur, guys?"

Singh and Aschenblum nodded.

"I want to second Singh's comment about underfunding," said Shaw. "I'm not a tech, but—" He hunched forward, his brow furrowed. "As far as security, or protecting proprietary developments go, this place is worse than lax."

Aschenblum nodded. "Ye-es," he said slowly, almost as though he were petting the word. "This is almost a make-work operation, Mr. Anan—a facade. Forgive me if I sound rude. Singh called it under-funded, but that's not so. It's, well, *stupidly* funded. The break room, for instance, is state of the art. The toilet facilities are cutting edge. But the actual equipment doesn't meet standards. Forgive me, but Chococoa was once—*remains*—a world-class brand. I've walked through the research and development sections of brands like that, and there's a *feel* to them. Something ambitious, aggressive. There's work to do here, but there isn't much being done.The people here are simply punching the clock."

Benjamin nodded. Nicola; it all came down to Nicola. Nicola and the marketing mindset Johanna had so often execrated. Nicola had redirected the vast bulk of Chococoa's resources into marketing and public relations. So long as the processes in the factory outside remained the same, so did the quality of the product. But funding had been drained from all other 'nonessentials' and so a slow corrosion had spread.

But there was nothing illegal, immoral or intrinsically destructive about that. Not in the short run, at least. It was a business decision. A decision to focus company efforts in one area instead of another. When the economy had been good, it proved a wise decision. No, more than that: when Nicola had been on *fire* to make Chococoa a world-class brand, when she *inspired* as well as directed, the entire company had felt it, had shared that visionary tone. Now the economy was not so good, and Nicola had curled herself into an uncommunicative shell. For some reason, Nicola had come to lack the flexibility, the *will*, to take the steps needed to push Chococoa forward. Something had happened to her. She no longer *drove* the company; she hovered over it. Over its demise.

Benjamin had picked up enough from Johanna's exaltation of supply chains to be able to see that there was nothing especially *wrong* with Chococoa's R&D; it was just weak, palsied. It needed an infusion of well-*directed* funds, new ideas. The leadership--Nicola--simply wasn't supplying them at the moment.

But there was a contradiction in what he was hearing. Was Nicola, apparently indifferent, even aware? Funds *were* going to R&D, he had been told. Why did nonessentials get them, yet the workroom floor not reflect it? Should he speak to Chris?

From what The Cult had said, the amounts spent were simply a matter of apparent thoughtlessness and waste. That mattered, but it was not the solution to Chococoa's problems. Benjamin was coming to the same conclusion here as Johanna in Ghana: there was simply a pervasive corrosion and lack of upkeep. Money thrown away for the sake of throwing it away.

He felt despair. Anger. For Benjamin, the company had always been more or less there in the background. Not till the last few days had he felt as though it were slipping away. All that his father had built up were dissolving, and it seemed as though he could do nothing about it.

Benjamin frowned. He had no right to fault Nicola; his own responses had been much the same. He had been building up his legal practice, giving the family business little attention, letting Chococoa slide. Now, at the last minute, when perhaps it was too late, he had begun to care. Silently he cursed himself.

I'm sorry, Papa.

Benjamin stood up.

"Let's go see Big Pharma," he said.

8

The girl ripped the hood off Jacob's head.

"*Hi* honey!" she said. "You have a nice nap, baby?"

She gave Jacob another ten-thousand-volt kiss.

He wanted to vomit.

"Huh, I think he gonna throw up!" the girl said.

She made a *Tsk!* Sound, deeply offended.

"Lot of people throw up after you hit them in the head," said the man. "Give him some water. It helps."

"What if he throw up on me while he's drinkin'! I don' want no puke on me!"

The man cursed all women from the beginning of creation, carefully excluding his mother, and filled a glass with water from a gallon container, and put the glass to Jacob's lips.

"Boy, you drink this up. Do it."

Jacob drank, and coughed, hard.

"What—" he said.

"Shut up," said the man. "I got to do some thinking."

The man walked out of Jacob's range of vision.

Jacob looked around. They seemed to be inside some kind of a makeshift living space inside the long box of a tractor-trailer. There were no windows, no toilet, but there were mattresses, piles of clothes everywhere, bongs, discarded bottles of beer and alcohol. At the far end, a DVD Player connected to a large-screen HDTV played *Star Wars: Revenge Of The Sith*.

"Want another kiss, pretty boy?" said the girl. "When Kofi here go outside to pee, I lock the door. Then we gonna do it *all!*"

Her giggle rose into a wild high screech.

"I cut off Pretty Boy's nose and ears and maybe you gonna do nothing," growled Kofi.

Jacob looked in the direction of the voice and saw a man in his thirties, lean and scarred, with thin hips and unusually broad shoulders. The body type rang a bell— "*You're* the man on the motorcycle! The one that rammed us," said Jacob.

Kofi looked over. "I tell you, shut up."

"You right, pretty boy! You got good eyes! Yep, Kwaku say 'Give 'em a scare, Kofi,' and Kofi give you a scare. Lucky you didn't go flyin'!"

"*Shut up!*" roared Kofi. "*Don't* you say that name. You mention the Devil and he comes!"

The girl turned to Jacob and rolled her eyes and stuck out her tongue. Her lips said, "Old Man Chicken Shit," but no sound came out. She gave Kofi a dirty look out of the side of her eyes.

Kofi opened up an old cell phone and talked into it. He waited a minute. A voice responded. Kofi talked. Suddenly Jacob could hear a voice shouting on the other end.

Kofi took a step over and slapped Jacob hard. He stuck the cell phone into his face.

"*Say your name, boy!*" yelled Kofi.

Jacob, disoriented, said, "M-my name is—I'm Jacob, Jacob Anan. Who—."

"*Jacob!*" screamed the voice on the other end. It was Johanna.

Kofi took the phone away. "We gonna talk again," he said. "You remember what I said. You *remember.*"

He cut her off.

Jacob became aware of a burning feeling across his wrists. He realized that he was seated in a metal chair, and that his wrists were bound with rope behind his back. His ankles, his legs, his waist, his chest were tied up tight with rope and bound to the chair too. He couldn't move.

"What do you people want with me?" he said.

Kofi stamped his foot and came over and gave Jacob a roundhouse slap across the face that nearly knocked him unconscious. "Did I say for you to *shut up!* Do you know what shut up *means?* I am *thinking!*"

"You need a brain for that, old man," said the girl, who shrieked as she ducked the punch that immediately flew her way.

"I kill your ass you say that again!" roared the man. "You hear me?"

He walked off to a pile of bottle of vodka, opened it, and fell down on a pile of clothes and lay back and had a long drink from the bottle. He closed his eyes.

The girl moved slowly back to Jacob's side. "He high," she whispered. "He grab you only 'cause he higher than a kite. Otherwise he don't *pee* unless Mr. Kwaku say so." The girl snorted. "Who care what Kwaku like? He don't say we *can't* grab you. Be a *man*, Kofi," she hissed. "Now he afraid Kwaku gonna come cut his balls off." She snickered. "*What* balls?"

"We're all gonna die!" moaned Kofi suddenly, his eyes still shut.

"See what I mean?" whispered the girl.

I'm in a lunatic asylum, thought Jacob.

No. No, thought Jacob. This Kofi was right. Stop. *Think.*

"You've, uh, you've kidnapped me. Is that correct?" whispered Jacob.

" 'Is that correct'?" She laughed, showing brilliant white teeth. "How dumb can you *be*, boy? You are dumber than you are pretty! *Hell yeah* we kidnap you.

Hell with *you*—we can live for a week if we just kidnap your *suit* and sell it on the street. *Sure* we kidnap you. Once your family hand over the money, it's goodbye *this* dump," she said. She whispered into Jacob's ear, and nibbled his earlobe. "It goodbye Old Man Kofi, too."

The dreadlocked girl got up and pulled a pear out of a plastic cooler and sat down by Jacob again and began peeling it with a paring knife, eating the strips. Jacob wondered if he would be the thing she carved next.

Focus, focus. Benjamin's mystery movies. There was a policeman—or was it Rumpole?—who said that kidnapped victims needed to befriend the kidnappers, to personalize their relationship.

Jacob looked at the girl and said, "You're too young and beautiful to be treated like this."

Her lips widened into a grin that stretched ear to ear.

"What's your name?" asked Jacob.

"Maria Magdalena Queen Of Heaven," she said.

"Lovely," said Jacob with all the sincerity he could muster. "A Catholic upbringing, then,"

"The nuns find me on the street, raise me. Gave me a name. I run off and Kofi grab me, put me out on the chocolate farms."

"Child trafficking,"

"I don't know. He get into trouble with Mr. Kwaku and Kwaku shut him down. I cut loose, try to go work for Chococoa. But they turn me down too. Too young. And I can't pass the drug test. I see Kofi on the street again and we connect. Live how we can. Kwaku, he take over everything, so we start running errands for Kwaku."

"Are you and he—um—a couple?"

Maria Magdalena covered her mouth and laughed. She shrugged and downed another chunk of fruit. "I do him. He do me. But he used to be a *man*." She sneered. "Now he just pee his pants every time he hear Kwaku name."

"And it's this Kwaku wants me kidnapped?"

"Who know what Kwaku wants? Kwaku like a god.

He say jump, people jump. He say die, people die. Kofi tell me Kwaku's boy say, 'hey Kwaku want you give Anan woman a little scare' and we get on our bikes outside and *do*."

The girl took a small plastic packet out of her tight back pocket and put it to one nostril, held the other, and snorted it. Then she reversed the process. As she put it back the eyes widened, and her irises too.

"Kwaku don't say nothing about *you*. He don't say leave you alone, either. Kwaku's boy pay us, we in the streets, we partying, we high, and then we see *you* walk by dressed like you Mr. Million Dollars. We see you go in that big building, and I say to Kofi, 'Kofi we *take* that boy and his family give *us* that million dollars. Then we fly away from here, *free* like birds. Like *birds!*' And Kofi higher even than *me*. He says yeah. Yeah!"

She spread her hands. "And now you here, Pretty Boy," said the girl. "Except now Kofi coming down. Now he like always. He think Kwaku gonna spank his dusty old ass." Her lip curled with contempt. "I *hate* that old man. You our ticket *out!* And that old fool too scared to take it. You my ticket *outta* here!"

She was speaking loud enough now for Kofi to hear. He sat up where he was lying, and blinked. For a moment Jacob was afraid he was going to come over and beat them both. Instead he rummaged around in his shirt pocket and took out a palmful of pills and washed them down with the bottle of alcohol that he was holding. He sat there with a dazed expression.

"Kwaku gonna kill us," he muttered. "Gonna *cut* us. Gonna cut us *up*."

"Be a *man*," screamed the girl.

"I told you to *shut up!*"

"*You* shut up!" screamed the girl.

"I kill you, girl!" roared Kofi, drug-intoxicated to the gills, staggering to his feet, and stomping over to smash her face with his massive fist.

The meth-eyed girl hissed like a puma set aflame

and, instead of retreating, threw herself out of control at the oncoming Kofi and plunged the paring knife into his chest. Once, twice.

He howled, and swatted her away with a single blow, and she leapt cat-like back on the older man. He fell backwards and she fell on top of him, stabbing him in the chest and abdomen over and over, till he pulled a gun out from under his shirt and shot five 9mm bullets into her body.

It picked her up to her feet, like invisible strings pulling up a puppet. She stood straight for a moment, did a jerky dance, rolled her head, and fell backwards flat as an ironing board, stone dead.

Kofi swore and wailed in pain and shot another final bullet into the air. "Won't *never... shut up...*" he said, and stretched back like a large old puma, and a large bubble of blood bloomed from his lips and did not pop.

And then Kofi was as dead as the girl.

Jacob had sat goggle-eyed and jaw hanging open through the entire proceedings, tied up in the chair.

"What?" he said. "What?"

He blinked at the dead bodies, jerked at his ropes. He couldn't move. He could not move at all.

"*What?*"

9

Benjamin knocked on the door leading to the facilities of Big Pharma. He noted that, unlike Chococoa's R&D there were a set of lockers near the door where personnel presumably suited up in biohazard suits. They had checked and a few were still in the lockers. He knocked again. After a few minutes had passed and still no one had responded, he nodded to Shaw, and Chococoa's Chief of Security pulled a chain on keys on his belt out, inserted one, and opened the lock. Benjamin opened the door and stepped in. The people with him followed.

The premises were in many respects a duplicate of the R&D section. Cafeteria in the back, sealed and isolated area in the center, processing machines surrounding it. The sealed block of space in the center had no vegetation, but only what appeared to be advanced chemistry equipment, and the processing units dripped not chocolate-like liquids, but pulped and sifted the rough minerals shipped in from Ghana into a fine dust. Machinery outside filled capsules with the refined product.

Nearly everyone on the floor dressed in either white or yellow versions of the biohazard suits. Benjamin was a bit taken aback at the comparative sterility, and immediately thought of bio-hazardous materials or chemical weapons. Popeye and his associates were far more bland, knowing as they did that the cost of a basic hazmat suit rarely exceeded sixty Euros, and casual attire was infinitely more risky. Only fools wore a tie near centrifuges. They were not surprised. The appearance of the place was what they expected.

What they did *not* expect was the body language of those inside. Work seemed to come to a complete halt. Everyone on the floor seems to stop and stare, dumbfounded.

Benjamin cleared his throat. "Good afternoon!" he announced. "May I speak to the Unit Manager, please?"

The people in the hazmat suits looked at one another. Who *were* these people?

A bulky figure in a hazmat suit strode quickly up and tore off his headgear. He had a large shaggy head, a grizzled beard, and an utterly appalled scowl.

"What the *hell* are you people doing in here?"

Benjamin removed an envelope from inside his Saville Row jacket and, with a sneer not unworthy of Rumpole himself, handed it over smartly, with all the majestic aplomb of an agent of the High Court serving a writ.

"I, sir, am Mr. Benjamin Anan, solicitor for Chococoa,

Ltd., which is the legal owner of this factory and these premises. The document you see gives us the right to inspect this area to see if it conforms to regulation standards for employee safety and— "

The man slapped the document away.

"I don't give a damn *what* you have. This area is *completely off-limits* to non-Pharma personnel. We have an agreement and I have direct orders! *No* one comes in without official approval."

"The document you have so cavalierly mis-handled, sir, provides exactly such approval."

"Not from *my* company, it doesn't," roared the man. "I would have been informed!"

"Your company signed the initial Agreement, sir. As you would know if you would bother to read the document."

"Get out!"

Shaw stepped in. The Chief of Security was quite as large as the Big Pharma man, and no less grizzled, and their own security man followed in tow. Shaw stood before the man in the hazmat suit face to face and said, "You can step aside. Or I can call in the security team for this entire factory and we can push you aside. You want that?"

The Big Pharma man sputtered.

Shaw turned his head to the rest of the team. "Go on. Go. Have a look."

"I'm calling our people!" said the man.

"Yeah, you do that," growled Shaw.

"You'll all be facing a law suit!" he shouted.

"Which we will win," said Benjamin. "Gentlemen, make your examination."

Popeye, Aschenblum and Singh detached themselves from the group and turned to the lockers. Popeye found an additional open marked locker inside the doors which he assumed, correctly, contained spare items including hazmat suits, and the trio donned them as the floor manager called out and began raging into his phone.

The three men floated seemingly randomly along the machinery and the monitoring devices and among various Big Pharma personnel, who seemed to regard them as strange but somewhat tolerable anomalies. They followed them with curious glances but were comparatively indifferent, unlike the floor manager, who flew into yet another fit of impotent but flamboyant rage as Aschenblum and Singh entered the sealed unit in the center.

Shaw followed the manager, stopping him from physically blocking them. They nearly came to blows. Only Benjamin, following Shaw, and re-stating Chococoa's legal right to review the premises, seemed to cool the confrontation back down to shouting levels.

As the conflict drew the attention of everyone on the floor, a smallish figure in a hazmat suit carrying a container of liquid entered quietly through the Pharma door and went to the interior lockers and stopped before a locker with a combination lock. The figure was completely overlooked as he opened the combination, opened the locker, and placed the container in the locker. He positioned his back to block anyone from seeing what he was doing. Then he unscrewed the container cap, tore off the mesh top, and put a box of matches on it. He lit one match, and inserted the end of it in the match box as the flame smoothly moved down the other end. The figure grabbed a few items off the shelf at the top of the locker, turned and left, shutting the Pharma door behind him.

The manager seemed finally to have gotten through to the appropriate person in Big Pharma when the locker exploded, spewing burning gasoline into the workspace.

Two passing workmen were splashed and caught fire. One staggered into a sifting device that caught and spat sparks as the man's hazmat suit caught in some gears. A muffled scream issued from the hazmat headgear. The sparks struck the flames, which burst higher, and floated across the air onto other workers and devices and chemical equipment. The latter began exploding too, risking a spread of toxic fumes.

Goodness! thought Benjamin.

Fire sirens began roaring. The sprinkler system tried to turn on—but failed, since the Big Pharma section had refused to allow any inspections since being acquired by the company. A washer failure that would have cost less than a dollar to replace rendered it useless.

The fire spread. Flasks and beakers sent shards slashing through the air. The figures in the hazmat suits began to panic, and several started to flee. Shaw broke away from the floor manager to find a fire extinguisher, but the Big Pharma people apparently kept them in a different place. He went back and called to the unit manager, who himself had run off at that point. The flames by now had formed a set of fluctuating walls, and Shaw grabbed Benjamin and shoved him toward the Pharma door and shouted, *"Get out of here! Everyone! Get everyone out of here! Now!"*

Through the clear walls of the sealed area containing Aschenblum and Singh, several Big Pharma workers in hazmat suits could be seen making wild gestures and pointing to the growing chaos outside.

They abandoned their equipment and ran.

Singh, Aschenblum, followed.

Sparse though the Big Pharma personnel were, the one door was soon crushed by fleeing individuals. Shaw, his face covered with a handkerchief, made a last loop around and fled too, next entering the R&D section and evacuating the personnel there as well. It was a wise move. The two units were separate, but not hermetically sealed. Shared electrical wiring overheated and the wiring then blew, as fire penetrated into the Chococoa R&D section as well.

Benjamin had already called the nearest Fire Department. It was not immediately nearby but arrived fairly rapidly and soon the fire was under control. No lives had been lost. Or so, at least, they assumed, as the unit manager could not be found, and Big Pharma had so far refused to take their calls or identify its personnel.

But whether or not Big Pharma would accept their call was not a great matter of concern at the moment.

What mattered was that the Big Pharma facility located on the premises of Chococoa, Ltd., was a smoking ruin.

And the Research & Development arm of Chococoa, Ltd., would be out of operation long past the deadline for sale.

Chapter Eight

Seven Principles

1

Johanna stood under the open sky in the center of Chococoa operations in Ghana. When Jacob's call came, and was cut off, she ran at once to the man from Interpol. She immediately next called the police. She tried to think think *think* of what to do next. And she just stood there, waiting, hoping, trembling with fear.

Jacob! she cried within herself.

What if he were dead? What if she had sent him to his death?

Workers went about their work, and business operations swirled around her. It meant nothing. She stood like a lone statue in the center of an immense desert.

And then a limousine pulled up to her.

It was long, black, gleaming, obviously owned by someone of wealth and importance. The glossily shining windows were impassably black. The running motor was almost supernaturally silent.

The door facing Johanna opened robotically, controlled either by servomechanisms or by magic.

She looked into the darkness inside, and saw nothing.

On the driver's side the door opened. A man stepped out. A Ghanaian, but huge and muscular, completely bald, standing there in an expensive business suit and dark sunglasses. He did not come around the vehicle or approach her. He simply moved his hand, gesturing forward at the open door beside her. *Your presence is requested. Come inside.*

Johanna felt herself drawn into the vehicle as though by an irresistible magnetism. *Jacob!* The word resonated inside her, but now somehow hallucinatory. Somehow, *somehow*, this had something to do with Jacob. She felt as though she were falling over a cliff.

Delicately, like Cinderella entering her magic carriage, she stepped into the limousine. The door closed magically, robotically. The driver re-entered and shut his door. The car pulled away.

2

"Mr. Anan," said Derek Eckland, Benjamin Anan's private investigator.

"Mr. Eckland," said Benjamin.

"I have some information for you."

Benjamin almost shrugged. What did it matter, at this point?

On the other hand, how could it get worse?

"Go on," said Benjamin, wearily.

"First of all—Nicola? She's clean. In fact spotless. I have to tell you, Mr. Anan, I rarely come across a person of interest in the business world whose fiscal picture is *this* clear and open. There isn't a cent out of place. She lives like a monk, entirely on her salary and on a few investments that were marked by no conflict of interest whatever, and which she recently closed out. She has no unexplained sources of income, nothing out of place whatsoever. It's almost amazing. There's only one thing that raises any concern."

"And that is?"

"Lately she's been putting a good deal of her money away—and I mean a *lot* of it, well over 90%—into Bitcoin and one or two other cryptocurrencies."

"That's odd, but why is it a concern?"

"Bitcoin's impenetrable. Once you've bought some and set it up—at least, if you do it right—no one can access it, no one can seize it, no one knows how much you've got in it or if you're the owner. It's completely bulletproof. If you do it right."

"She's putting her money into a Bitcoin account rather than a bank account. Quirky, but what of it?"

"Very few people do it, and even fewer know how. Presumably she's doing it to keep her funds secure and anonymous. But why?"

"Well, why?"

"I don't know."

Benjamin found it hard to summon up enough interest even to pursue it. He sat in the boardroom at Chococoa, with a few of the others who had escaped the fire, waiting for Nicola and Naomi to consume them in another fire: the appropriate flames of their wrath.

It's the end, thought Benjamin. *The company's finances are already in trouble. A major fire? Chococoa is dead. And I'm the one that's killed it.*

He pulled himself together. "The bottom line, Mr. Eckland, is that regardless of where she keeps her money, if it's her money, and if she's earned it honestly, she can put it wherever she likes. You say her personal financial record is clean?"

"Immaculate."

"Then that's all there is to say. I thank you for your services."

He prepared to hang up.

"There's just one thing," interjected Eckland.

Benjamin paused.

"What?"

"The woman's certainly well educated, and

intelligent. But she's not a geek. It takes a certain level of computer savvy to do what she's done. I asked myself where she learned to do what she did? Or who did it for her?"

"And the answer is—?"

"It has to be your Finance guy. Chris. I asked around, and apparently he has a degree in Computer Science from Vancouver. He took that and applied it to a Financial Masters in Canada, and ended up programming financial databases and transactional apps for a number of companies before working here. He's the only one in Nicola's circle I can see who could reasonably be expected to have tutored her in Bitcoin."

"Well, that was certainly very nice of him. Is there anything else, Mr. Eckland?"

Benjamin could almost feel Eckland shake his head on the other end of the call.

"Mr. Anan. *Nicola* is as clean as new-fallen snow. *Chris* is as clean as a row of Yorkshire outhouses."

"You investigated Chris as well?"

"That's right. And *he* is interesting."

"How so?"

"Once upon a time, back when he was in Vancouver, he was *very* heavily involved with Silk Road."

"And what's that?"

"One of the first, and most legendary, of the online drug exchanges. The founder is currently in jail for life, but back in its heyday it was the online world's leading drug marketplace. Heroin, Ecstasy, LSD, prescription, experimental medical drugs—you name it, Silk Road sold it. Payment in Bitcoin exclusively."

"You mean Nicola—."

"No, there's no evidence Nicola ever knew what Silk Road was. On the other hand, there *is* evidence, a ton of it, that Chris was a Silk Road power user and very much a member of the community. It's probably where he picked up his expertise in Bitcoin."

Benjamin considered. "All this tells me is that back

when he was in college Chris consorted with drug users and may have used some himself. That's hardly unique behavior, Mr. Eckland. After all, he couldn't have been *that* involved with the worst drugs imaginable if he managed to score his degree and master his undeniable skills at the same time."

"But that isn't all."

"Continue."

"*His* financial picture is secretive and erratic. He seems to have been getting additional funds from unknown sources, and his outgoing funds, what I could trace, are as cryptic as Nicola's. I don't know where his funds are going either, and I'm not suggesting they're going to the same place, or that there's any connection with Nicola's. Who knows, he may simply be dealing drugs to a small assortment of his friends. But he's definitely doing *something* he wants to keep secret."

"Is he embezzling?"

"I have no evidence of that. Yet."

"Is he engaging in any criminal activity at the moment?"

"He certainly *has* engaged in criminal activity, though I don't know whether he could be successfully prosecuted at this point. And I have no *hard* evidence that he's now engaging in criminal activity. No hard evidence yet."

"If you think that, no doubt others do. Is there a possibility Chris is being blackmailed?"

"I don't know."

Benjamin nodded.

"Find out, Mr. Eckland," he said.

3

He thought, of all things, of Nicola. Jacob had had thoughts about Nicola before, thoughts that he tried to shoo away, but Nicola had a way of saying things that stuck. When asked why she adopted some particular course, her response often as not was, *Because I am a rational human being*. It was intended to shut down discussion. This was the most reasonable course of action, at least as Nicola saw it. End of deliberation. Start of execution.

But the phrase came to Jacob now. *I am a rational human being*. It came to him, and he repeated it over and over, like a mantra. Because his desperation was bleeding into panic, and he had to stop it, stop it cold, if he wished to survive.

I am a rational human being, he whispered to himself. *I am a rational—"*

A rat emerged from under the mass of rags that now served as a burial bier for Kofi, and sniffed Kofi's ear and began to chew at it.

Jacob wanted to vomit.

But instead he repeated his mantra, till he finally stopped repeating it and asked what a rational human being would actually do in his situation. Answer: assess it soberly.

He looked around. He appeared to be on the inside of a long trailer, inside which the man and woman who had brought him here seemed to be squatting. Therefore, he thought, it was probably abandoned somewhere or otherwise isolated, or possibly in a garbage dump. The HDTV was still playing *Revenge Of The Sith* on DVD. There was no sign of a Cable supplier. Possibly they were in the forest. All the drug and music paraphernalia suggested that they had no concerns about disturbing the neighbors.

Conclusion: no one would hear him scream for help.

He screamed for help anyway. You never knew.

But no one came.

OK, he thought. *All right. What's the worse thing that could happen? I can't get out of this chair. In two days, maybe three, without water I die of dehydration. How likely is that?*

He had no idea. But if he were in an isolated

location—a reasonable enough assumption, if that's where you're keeping your kidnap victim—it was also reasonable that no one would turn up for the next several days. Just sitting there could be fatal.

I have to get out. Now, while I still have the strength.

He was tied up. He might have been able to break the chair by rolling around if it were made of wood. But it was metal. Could he move anyway? Yes. He tried rocking the chair side to side. The base of the legs scraped against the tractor-trailer floor. A half hour of effort moved him forward several inches. But where was he going? Even it the trailer door were open, and not locked, so long as he was tied to the chair, all he would do is fall to the ground. If the mosquitoes in this country had taught him one thing, it's that lying on the ground for hours would leave his bones picked clean.

Come on, he said to himself. *Think. Think!*

There had to be a way…

The cell phone!

If he could flip it open, he could find some way to place a call. His hands were bound, but the floor was a mess. All sorts of things were on it. Was there anything he could use? Yes! There! Next to a box of take-out—a chopstick! If he knocked the cell phone to the floor, he could open it with his tongue, and if he could drag himself to the chopstick and put it in his mouth, he could press the number buttons on the phone and place a call to Johanna. Even to home!

Home, he thought. The thought of fish and chips brought tears to his eyes.

It was a plan.

Slowly, quarter-inch by quarter-inch, he pulled his chair closer to the box and the cell phone atop it.

4

The inside of the car was perfectly silent. Johanna

sensed that the vehicle was moving, yet there seemed to be no vibration, and no sound penetrated from the world outside. A pane of black glass separated those in the rear from the driver up front. It was spacious, luxurious, comfortable, all silver and black leather, exquisitely expensive. There was an inset light in the roof, and it came on. It was positioned so that the light shone on Johanna, and darkened the space behind it.

In that space Johanna could detect a shape. A man.

"Johanna Anan," said the man. "This *is* a pleasure. Young lady, I am your greatest admirer."

The voice was rich and deep and Shakespearean, obviously polished, strangely frightening. And there was something *wrong* with it, as though it were coming from a damaged throat, or a throat that had been damaged and repaired, replaced with something metallic.

She knew the question to ask should have been, *Who are you?*, but instead she broke down, and begged.

"*Save my brother!*" she said. She broke into tears.

The shape in the darkness seemed to consider this. Then the rich strange voice returned.

"Yes, I'd heard that Jacob had been kidnapped. An unfortunate distraction. It was not done at my instruction, and I cannot guarantee that your brother is alive, or unharmed. But *if* your brother is alive, be assured that I will find him and return him. You would like that, would you not, Johanna?" he asked gently.

"Yes," she sobbed.

The voice seemed to smile. "Consider it done. Better yet: consider it a glimpse of what *can* be done."

"I don't understand what you mean," said Johanna, her tears still running.

"You don't need to understand," said the voice, delicately, as though petting her. "What you need to understand is this: I have decided to take a new direction. The caterpillar sheds its cocoon to become a butterfly. So too with one's activities. Periodically one must shed one's skin, renew oneself, press forward toward new shores. Do you understand?"

"No," she said. "I don't understand a thing you're talking about. I just want *my brother back*. I want him back safe and alive."

"I envy you," said the voice. "Your affection. Your loyalty. My brothers and sisters are all dead. I have no one left to lose. No one, and nothing."

He leaned forward into the light, till the light revealed his face.

"I am Kwaku," he said.

Johanna recoiled and *screamed*. She screamed again, clawing at the door for a handle to escape.

Kwaku leaned back into the darkness, and waited.

"*So* predictable," he said. "I'm afraid you haven't passed your first test very well, young lady."

"My first *test*? What do you mean, my first test?"

"You are being interviewed. If you pass the interview, your brother continues to live. You continue to live too. If you fail, well… "

It was like a slap across the face. When she first stepped into the car she was still half-stunned. She had gotten in because some intuition had told her—correctly!—that she would find an answer inside. Instead she had found… what? Some kind of monstrosity on whom Jacob's life, and her life, depended. And what had she done? She begged. She *sniveled*. She brushed the tears from her eyes with a kind of fury.

"Who are you?" she said coldly.

"I am Kwaku."

"And what exactly is that?"

"Ah: an intelligent comment at last. Yes, labels mean nothing. *What* am I? An excellent question."

The back of the seats whirred and suddenly two panels slid out, each containing glasses. Between them a third long row slid out next, with slices of fresh orange, lemon and lime, small cubes of ice, and bottles. Kwaku's hand reached out and grasped a Cointreau, and he poured it into his glass along with some ice.

"Do help yourself, Miss Anan. It steadies the nerves."

"I'm fine, thank you," she said, her voice barely in control.

"Oh, go ahead. It may be your last, you know. Life is nothing if not uncertain."

"*Get to the point,*" she said sharply.

Kwaku laughed. "That's better. That's the Johanna I'm used to."

Kwaku took a long and thoughtful sip.

"You see, Miss Anan," he said, "I am what is known as a supervillain. You know; those fellows in the James Bond movies, the ones with scars and metal claws for hands and slithering pet snakes? The ones dispatching hordes of slavish killers and pitiless assassins? The ones out to rule the world? Well, that's me. Except I don't really want to rule the world. Just Ghana. And possibly parts of Europe and the Caribbean. It's easier than you think. You simply build up a major criminal enterprise, eliminate your competitors, bribe enough police officials and politicians to do what you say, and *voilà*—you are in charge of your own little transnational domain. Do you follow me so far?"

Johanna nodded.

"My predecessors and competitors—now sadly deceased—were petty creatures, driven by greed and ego. Once sated with money and sensuality, they grew fat and comfortable. And then, naturally, they became dead. They were not men of vision. *I* am a man of vision. I want Ghana to be wealthy and prosperous. A star-faring nation. A nuclear power, feared and respected. A land free of poverty. A place where children are not enslaved. Where they do not have to sell drugs, or themselves, on the streets. Is that not a *worthy* goal, young lady? But all that will never be achieved, Miss Anan, all the existing horrors will keep happening, because Ghana is full of very bad, very greedy, very cruel, very *weak* individuals. Once I kill the vast majority of these superfluous parasites and put the rest under my iron heel, that will no longer be the case. I will be able to shape the nation—and a few other nations—as I wish."

Johanna was not deeply religious, but out of nowhere, she found herself saying, "The Bible says, 'Do not do evil that good may come of it.' "

"The Bible says that?" said Kwaku, surprised. He sipped his Cointreau. "So what?"

5

It took the better part of an hour. But Jacob finally managed to drag himself over the cardboard box with the phone on it. All he had to do now was to knock it over to the floor, tip himself over as well, pick the nearby chopstick up with his mouth, open the cell phone lib, and press a number.

But—

Next to the phone lay a bong and a votive candle. The bong was irrelevant, and the candle stank. But the candle was *lit*. And if the candle fell onto the pile of clothes, the clothes would catch fire and the trailer would fill with smoke and flame. And Jacob would die.

The box was a plain cheap cardboard box, the sort in which whiskey bottles came encased. It barely came up even to Jacob's knee. He could wait for the candle to die out naturally, but how long did candles take to die out? Days? He tried blowing it out, but he was too far away. The flame guttered but remained strong. He tried spitting, but again it was too far away, and his aim stank worse than the candle's cloying apricot smell.

I'm so damned close, he thought. *So close!*

There was no other way.

He had to nudge the box. If he could knock the phone off without knocking off the candle too, he'd be free. He could escape. If he knocked the candle off instead...

If he knocked the candle off instead, he'd die.

6

"But I digress," said Kwaku. "In the course of building up my criminal operations, two things happened that have given me considerable pause. One: I found myself taking over a number of conventional businesses and having to run them profitably. Two: I found myself applying their benchmarks to my criminal operations, and I found the latter wanting. *Badly* wanting. Really, Miss Anan, you have no idea how hard it is to recruit and keep competent criminal talent. Or build brand loyalty for *your* illegal drug and not some cheap parody brewed in a basement. Or to build a supply chain that the authorities don't raid, or competitors don't bomb. Slowly, inch by inch, I have dragged myself to the preeminent peak in local criminality. But what I've found here at the top is not unrestrained efficient power, but a vast number of sloppily bumbling, almost comic criminal operations, and aboveground operations needing constant micromanagement.

"In short," he concluded, "I need a supply-chain analyst."

He topped off his drink with an additional slice of lime.

"Are you sure you won't have a Cointreau, Miss Anan? We have Drambuie as well."

"Are you offering me a *job?*"

"Not at all. I am merely interviewing you for a job. I was very taken by your pitched debates with Nicola Cavalcanti some time ago. You seemed, at moments, almost her match, although from a completely different angle. Mind you, I've learned a great deal from Nicola. A *great* deal. You can't imagine how well I've branded myself locally. The name Kwaku is synonymous with terror. People literally believe I'm some sort of demon, and not the savior that I *truly* am. And I barely had to kill a few score of people that badly needed killing to do it! But I believe I have drained the cup of branding dry. I have new problems. It is high time I found new mentors."

"You heard Nicola and myself arguing? Where?"

"Your firm is one of those in which I have an interest. It goes without saying that your offices are under my surveillance. It wasn't for purposes of spying on your debates as such. I simply wanted to learn how a successful formal business operated. What better way than simply to watch?"

"And Nicola *works* for you?"

Kwaku chuckled. *"She* doesn't think so. Ah, the delusions of women! Your firm is a conduit, Miss Anan, one of several that allows me to launder some part of the money my drug operations generate. The funds are sent to Chococoa under the guise of being charitable donations that your firm generously helps manage, and from there they are redirected to a variety of ostensible charities that are simply masks which allow the funds to circulate above ground. You see why a supply chain specialist is needed? Such ridiculous complexity."

"And Nicola assists."

"Nicola looks the other way. In return for her life. And all of yours. But the feisty little poodle never stops barking at me. It's a rationalization to bandage her wounded ethical posturings, of course. I allow it because she entertains me. Immensely. I am not yet done with Nicola," he said. "However, the firm used to launder the funds is simply coming under too much official attention."

"Freedom For The Children," said Johanna. Now she finally understood Nicola's connection to the organization.

"Yes. It was useful at the time. But your friend from Interpol is not the only dog sniffing at its heels. Since then I've created several parallel such organizations, so it's no longer critical to my larger operations. Thus, I believe the time has come to close this particular shop. Of course there's also the matter of *your* little firm and its recent stumblings."

"*You're* the mystery buyer," she whispered Johanna. "*You're* the one behind everything. It's all so you can take over."

Kwaku snorted. "Such vanity. I *have* been half-tempted to take it over now and again, you know. Mostly out of sentiment. But is the return on investment really worth it, compared to the returns from more profitable businesses I can acquire—not to say from the drugs, prostitution, assassinations, political pay-offs, that are my mainstay?" He waved his hand. "Pah."

"It's not you?"

"I have other resources, and better ones."

"Then why did you kidnap my brother?"

"I did *not* kidnap your brother. Although I believe I know who did. Greedy underlings, alas. See the recruiting issues I face? I sent them out to give your motorcycle a little *tap* earlier."

"That was you?"

"I thought our conversation would go more smoothly if I dangled you off a cliff beforehand. I find that discussions go more smoothly once the other person knows I can make them die violently with a snap of my fingers. It was a way of to remind Nicola of the same. She needs a regular reminder." He sighed. "But the motorists I employed likely thought they could make a little extra without the Boss noticing. They always do. Who knows better than I?" he said, with a trace of sadness.

"Then you can find them! And Jacob!"

"I expect I can. I expect he's well. You tell me you heard his voice. I doubt they're stupid enough to take his life."

"Then do it!"

"In exchange for—?"

Johanna struggled to find words.

"What do you *want?*"

"What do I want? Why, you, Johanna. I want you, of course."

7

It took Jacob nearly an hour to get close enough to the box to be able to touch it with his foot. If he simply tipped the chair over and crashed into the box, the candle would go flying onto the clothes, and that would be the end. If he put his entire leg next to the box, nothing would happen. He was tied up so tightly he would have to shift his entire weight each time, and could not be sure of how strongly his impact would affect the items atop the box.

So he positioned his foot right next to the box and nudged it. There was little visible effect.

But there was *some*.

He tried again. And again. And again. And again.

The items moved closer to the edge.

All the items. The cell phone, the bong and the candle.

He nudged the box again, and again, and *again*. His forehead broke out in a sweat. The trailer was not air-conditioned. There was a standing fan at the far end, but set to off. He couldn't reach it. *It must be a hot day outside,* he thought, adding a curse under his breath. It was certainly hot inside. A bead of sweat sank down and curled into his eye. The salt made his eye tear and smart. He nudged the box again. And again. And again.

Minutes passed that felt like hours that felt like days. The objects crawled, crawled like dying snails, closer to the edge of the box, and Jacob *could not* isolate the cell phone from the others. As the phone came closer to the edge, so did the candle. The closer they came to the edge, the less Jacob could tell which would go over first.

Again he nudged the box, and again, and again, and again.

The bong went over, falling onto a set of the late Kofi's socks and soiled underwear.

Now there were only the cell phone and the burning candle.

Jacob stared at them, almost burning into the items with his eyes. He had never been so absorbed, so focused on anything in his entire life. Both the phone and the candle were near the edge. If he kept going, both would sit farther and farther *over* the edge, and *one* would fall first.

Which? If staring could have estimated it, his intense expression would have given him the answer. But it couldn't. There was nothing to do but keeping going.

Please, he whispered to God, *please let it be the phone.*

Again he nudged the box, and again, and again.

And this time the phone seemed to wobble on the edge.

His heart leapt up.

He shut his eyes, concentrated, and nudged the box.

Again the phone wobbled.

He nudged again and the phone wobbled—and so did the burning candle.

"No!" he screamed, *willing* the candle to stand still.

The candle's wobbling… gradually… stopped.

Both phone and candle were sitting over the very edge of the case. What would the next tap do? Send the phone over into the clothing, or the candle? Should he stop? Jacob felt a sickness in the bottom of his stomach, a sickness so intense he could no longer control himself.

Vomit spat from his mouth.

He turned his head away at the last moment. The box remained undisturbed. The two items sat on the knife edge.

All it needed was a tap to send one or the other over. Or both.

Tears of anger, pain, fury spilled from his eyes.

Am I about to die?

He shut his eyes, gained control of himself. A hard coldness spread through his chest, his arms, his legs and feet. Yes, maybe he *was* going to die. But he wasn't going to die crying like a baby with the taste of vomit in his mouth. He wasn't going to sit there too paralyzed with fear to move. He thought of the example of his father, his brother, his sister. He was an Anan. If this was the time for him to die, he would die *well.*

He put the side of his foot against the box, muttered a prayer to God from the very bottom of his heart, and pulled his foot back to nudge the box one final time.

One—

Two—

Thr—

The phone fell over into the clothing without Jacob even touching the box.

8

"You want *me?*"

"Oh, not in a carnal sense. Don't flatter yourself, young lady. I can have the company of dozens of women willing to do whatever loathsome thing I please with the wave of a hand. Women whose beauty renders your own feral charms analogous to those of an aardvark. I do not want your body. I want your *input.* The complexity of my various operations is becoming... challenging. I've learned all I can from Nicola, but her gifts are specific to marketing. Not that I wish to dismiss them, not all. She is a brilliant woman. Most people think of crime in such crude terms; Nicola helped me appreciate it for what it is—an art form. Misdirection, showmanship, the unexpected, timing, symbolism. Oh yes—a high art indeed. I cannot tell you the *horror* I strike in the hearts of people here in Ghana. It's useful, but what I really need to do at this point is simply to run things *better,* more profitably, more efficiently. You wish to do it on a tiny scale of your trivial business. I wish to do it on a vaster canvas involving multiple businesses both criminal and legitimate. Nationally. Internationally. I require expert assistance. Professional assistance."

Johanna considered his offer. For less than a microsecond.

"No," she said.

"Oh, *come*. Johanna—the supply chain obsessive! You disappoint me. Why bother with your one failing firm and its petty little set of operations when you could be analyzing dozens? And *what* operations! Ones not bound by laws or regulations in the least. Operations whose functions are hidden in shadows! Why, drugs alone are a masterful area for your art. The raw materials; their processing; their pricing and distribution. Are these not supply chains too? Are they not a challenge? Unique? Fascinating? *Diversification*, my dear! *Multiple* streams of income! *Multiple* chains of supply! *Multiple* ventures and operations! What octopus restricts himself to one tentacle? Why bother with your piddling little chocolate bars when you could be shaping the destiny of your nation? Your *homeland?* Surely you have at least an *abstract* interest in the supply chain problems I present?"

Despite herself, Johanna had to nod. Kwaku was indeed making an interesting proposal. Supply chains fascinated her, and he was offering her a chance to explore the most complex assortment imaginable. She *did* have an interest, an abstract interest. Yes, it *was* fascinating…

"No," she said.

Kwaku sighed. "My dear. I'm not asking you to sell your soul."

"Yes, you are," she said.

"And is that too high a price to pay for your brother's life?"

Johanna said nothing; and then her discipline buckled. She broke into tears. Loud, uncontrolled, agonized, wretched sobbing.

Again, Kwaku sighed. The shape in the darkness removed a white silk handkerchief from his suit and tossed it to her.

"There, there. Blow your nose, girl. We'll get your little brother back. You don't have to sell your soul to the Devil."

She looked at the figure in the darkness, her eyes glistening.

"But in return can you *at least* favor me with some polite conversation?"

Johanna wiped her nose.

She nodded.

"I have *grave* organizational challenges. Structural challenges. I am forced to work with lice who routinely steal and who improvise mindlessly, doing things against my wishes—such as kidnapping your brother. Turnover is constant. I cannot recruit employees from agencies, or view their resumes on LinkedIn. In my drug operations, at least, they are often addicts with prison or psychiatric records."

"You have a staffing problem," said Johanna.

"*You* have a capacity for understatement."

Johanna brushed the tears away from her eyes.

"Have you segmented your customer base?" she said.

"What do you mean?"

"Well—sorry, first I need to ask whether you've properly isolated your business operations. You tell me you've taken over normal, legitimate, privately and publicly owned, business operations?"

"Yes."

"You don't hire schizophrenic drug addicts to run those."

"No."

"So a part of your operations function normally, without staffing issues. May I ask if those operations supply the majority of your revenues?"

"Not as *yet*. But that may change by the end of this year. Frankly, the income from banks and credit derivatives *eclipse* that of normal criminal activities."

"You own a bank?"

"Several. To be precise: I *control* several banks. I personally own nothing."

"That must be helpful when tax time comes around."

"It is. But this doesn't address the problems I face in drug operations."

"It does suggest that you may want to transition further and more rapidly into non-criminal activities such as banking."

"You clearly have little understanding of banking if you characterize it as non-criminal."

"As for your drug operations specifically, again, have you segmented your customer base?"

"In what way?"

"I'm assuming that the end buyers of your products are different consumer groups. Your street addicts are very different from elite professional cocaine users, correct?"

"Very."

"Are the distributors you use to supply elite users as, uh, troublesome?"

Kwaku considered. "No. As a rule, the distributors I employ are of the same social strata as the users. In fact, the buyers who become users generally provide the pool from which distributors are drawn."

"This, then, is where the staffing chain begins," said Johanna. "Let me ask you this. Which market segment—which group of buyers—supplies the most revenue?"

"Initially, street users. Increasingly, the elite users."

"Classically, this is what as known as the first of the 'Seven Principles,' a kind of road map of supply chain analysis. You ask yourself what sorts of people buy your product, and if they're very different sorts of buying communities, you adapt your product differently to each. You have different groups of customers. You serve them differently?"

"Yes, but they also serve different *ends*."

"What do you mean?""

"There are street rats, for instance, who rob homes

and break skulls and spend the money on an immediate fix. They end up in prisons or graveyards rather quickly. By contrast, elite users are often trendy, smug young men and women whose prestigious parents serve the government, or, offshore, pilot the EU. They require different handling. But then they provide different sorts of return, as well. Those at the bottom see themselves as having little to lose. They kill for me, prostitute themselves, are a constant supply of cash in small denominations. And cash flow *is* king, you know."

"The elite?"

"They pay better, mostly for the delusion of quality in the drugs they purchase. But once addicted, or subject to blackmail, *they* supply influence. The benefits from *that* pale beside the street cash flows."

"You need to adapt your chain of operations to address each market segment uniquely."

"How so?"

"Focus more on the one that's profitable, and less on the one that's troublesome. Or outsource. You say that you... eliminated your competition?"

"Yes."

"Perhaps you should employ them rather than eliminate them. Set up the equivalent of franchises. Instead of killing a competitor, allow them to, as it were, *lease* a particular area in return for a percentage. You still generate profit. You just don't have to deal with the underclass that provides it directly."

"Lieutenants become over-ambitious."

"Eliminate them *then*. You manufacture drugs as well as sell them, I assume? You're not the middle-man."

"No. I have special facilities that make the substances my operation sells."

"What about your logistics networks?"

"Please clarify."

"Principle number two. Your warehouses."

"We have a several such locations."

"Where?"

"All in Ghana."

"Small? Large?"

"Large would be foolish. The authorities do, on rare occasions, stage raids. Largely for show, so as to display a degree of muscle. But losing a *major* facility could be costly. I've arranged it so there are several spots."

"Do they house drugs indiscriminately?"

"What do you mean?"

"From your description, I assume the different consumer groups favor different drugs."

"Yes. Street people favor methedrine, heroin, hashish. The elites, cocaine, Ecstacy."

"Are your storage facilities serving the street people near the cities where they live? Is that where you principally store that market segment's preferred drugs? Are the storage facilities serving the elite near the elite?"

"No," said Kwaku.

"They should be. Faster delivery time. Also, separating the types of product ensures that you don't fail your consumers as a whole if a facility is raided."

"Hm," said Kwaku.

"What about demand planning? Do you listen to market signals?"

"Meaning?"

"Principle number three. Be alert to emerging demand. Do your markets have trends?"

"Oh, definitely. Once marijuana and psychedelics were all the rage. Then meth. Opioids seem to be the coming thing. Culturally, America ever points the way. Alas."

"Are the trends predictable?"

"To a degree. We don't do focus groups, obviously."

"You can see what new products are selling in other markets. You can keep your ears open and listen to what's being said on the street. Do you, or don't you?"

"Not systematically."

"Start. Improve your data-gathering. Do you sell online?"

"Of course."

"You can plot demand simply by seeing who buys what and in what proportion. We can presume that a rise in the online market demand will reflect offline market demand. Moreover, you can apply Principle number four."

"Which is?"

"Differentiate the product. If market signals suggest increase in a particular kind of product—narcotics instead of stimulants, say—customize your product to meet that demand. Present them as Ghanaian opioids, not as some new American product. That is to say, if you can manufacture them here."

"We can."

"Do you?"

"Opioids? No."

"Does anyone? That's principle number five. Don't do what someone else can do more cheaply and effectively. Or, to put it another way, outsource strategically. If Nigerian suppliers can bring you material to sell here, why set up a whole new manufacturing operation?"

"I like to have everything under my direct control."

"That's a personal decision, not a business decision. In business, you work with others. You present a clear case that shows that doing something you want them to do is profitable for them as well."

"That is not how Kwaku operates."

"Then find a lieutenant who does. Look, you want to achieve a *goal*, right? Is violence always your first and only option to achieve it? Is it the *best* way, with the least negative consequences? If you can make a persuasive case for mutual benefit, you can achieve your goal without spilling blood."

Johanna could hear the smile in Kwaku's voice. "You're trying to *manipulate* me, aren't you?" He laughed. "And you're doing it very well!"

"You say you're 'taking over' businesses," said Johanna. "If you want to operate them, you have to learn to make persuasive mutually beneficial deals. You have to present plans that show that *this* undertaking will gain *this* business advantage. Then people will sign on. If you don't—"

"If I don't, I will end up with more Chococoas, where I pull the strings of the puppets who run the business, but business slowly collapses, because the puppets only dance out of fear. Hm."

Kwaku was silent for several moments.

"Principle six?" he said at last.

" 'Establish IT support for multi-level decision-making,' "

Kwaku whistled. "And that means?"

"Connect up. Every last person of importance in every one of your operations has a smartphone. You can know where they are, what they're doing, you can pick their brains for ideas, you can build a *simulation model* that shows your entire operation functioning in real time, that responds predictively to variable input, you can make informational resources available to every member of the team, you can—"

"I can create a digital entity that will allow the authorities, or a clever enough competitor, to take my entire set of operations down with one stroke."

"You can compartmentalize it. Secure it. You can get computer security people. Our Financial Officer used to do something like that. Really, this isn't worth discussing. You can't run any kind of business operation nowadays, legal or illegal, with a notepad and pencil, or out of your head. You have to digitize. The market is *information*. You have to find some way to gather and summarize that information so you can see *what's happening,* and what happens when you make changes and improvements. IT is the best way. The only way."

"That is not easy to do when the majority of your operations are in the shadows."

"Then kidnap Bill Gates' little brother!" she exploded. "It's what you *have to do*. Somewhere someone needs the ability to get a clear view of the flow of *all* products, services, sequence of operations, information, of *what's actually going on*. How are you supposed to run a business if you don't know what anyone is *doing?*"

Kwaku was silent.

"Noted," he finally said. "And the last principle?"

"Metrics. Benchmarks. Obviously. You can't reach a goal if you don't set one. You need to set *measurable criteria* all along your operations every step of the way. How long does it take for your supplies to arrive? How long are they on the market on average before they begin to be exhausted, and you need more? Exactly how much profit does each separate product produce? Which market segments are most profitable, which ones are least? Business is mathematics. Measure everything. Crunch the numbers. The numbers will tell you exactly where you are and the direction you're going. The numbers will also tell you if you're reaching the goals you've set for yourself and your company."

Kwaku was silent.

They rode on for several miles more in the black soundless vehicle. How quickly were they going? Johanna could not tell. Where were they? Was she being taken to Jacob? Was she being kidnapped along with him?

The silence coming from the shape in the darkness grew thicker and more oppressive.

When she could no longer stand it, Johanna asked, "Are you taking me to my brother?"

"No," said Kwaku, replacing his empty glass in the inset panels, which closed automatically. "I have a previous appointment."

He snapped his fingers.

The car door beside Johanna popped all the way open.

The driver made an instant, impossibly sharp, left turn.

Johanna went flying.

Blinding light, noise, shouts, curses, screaming brakes.

She had been thrown onto the pavement of a cross-section in downtown Accra. Sunlight poured down on her. Traffic surrounded her. Horns blared. People stared from the sidewalks as she rose to her feet. The driver had been going just slowly enough to cast her out without injury, only minor scrapes and abrasions, and he had pivoted at just the right spot to keep her from being crushed or struck by oncoming traffic. The traffic had screeched to avoid hitting her regardless, and the string of rear-end collisions formed a virtual caterpillar of cursing, swearing motorists radiating around her.

She stood in the center of the discordant sunlit Accra chaos; wonderingly; dazed.

Her cell phone rang.

She took it out of her pocket as she stood there in the center of Accra traffic, motorists cursing as they drove around her. She held the phone to her ear, too stunned to move away.

"Hello?"

"Johanna?"

"Hi, Benjamin."

"Hi," said Benjamin. "Johanna… "

"Yes, Benjamin?"

"Johanna… Jo, we did the inspections… "

"Yes, Benjamin."

"And… and it was a disaster. A *disaster.* There was an explosion. A fire. The Pharma section is—it's gone. All burned away. It spread to R&D. It's a total loss. We're certain to be sued. Johanna, I'm *so sorry...*"

She nodded.

"Jacob's been kidnapped," said Johanna.

A Ghanaian police officer on a motorcycle drove to Johanna and asked her, in *Twi*, what the hell she was doing.

"Jacob's been kidnapped," said Johanna to Benjamin again, and, blinking, put the phone back into her pocket.

9

When the cell phone plopped onto Kofi's soiled underwear, Jacob's heart exploded with a joy he had never known or felt in the course of his entire lifetime. His body became electrified with a gratitude to God that lit him with renewed strength, a radiance, that coursed through him like sunlight. He sobbed aloud, unable to contain himself. And then he swept the tears from his face with a violent jerk of his head, pushed back his chair, tilted it in the direction of the chopstick on the floor, and hurled the chair and himself over.

His head struck the floor. He barely noticed. His limbs were on fire, his entire body felt supercharged. He jerked and jerked and jerked again and in minutes his lips closed over the chopstick and seconds later his teeth clamped over it hard. He began making a slow clockwise turn on the floor turning his head in the direction of the phone and then inch by inch, centimeter by centimeter by painful centimeter, he edged himself closer to the phone.

He could *see* it. It lay there in front of him. In ten more minutes of slow painful crawling he could plant the end of chopstick beyond it and pull it toward him, and then it would be next to his mouth and he could open it and press Johanna's number and—

And the candle fell off the edge of the box and into the pile of clothes.

No...! he thought, stricken. *No!... Don't... don't burn...*

But thin wisps of smoke were already starting to rise from the place that the candle had fallen.

In moments there would be tapers of flame.

And in minutes after that the entire trailer would be a fireplace, an inferno of conflagration.

Tears appeared in Jacob's eyes.

Then he mastered himself, and with an expression of great dignity, rested the side of his head against the floor.

He closed his eyes.

Chapter Nine

To Nicola

1

Moments earlier, before Johanna had called, Benjamin had been sitting in the boardroom. Stunned. Dumbfounded. Naomi would appear shortly. What was he to say? What had *happened?*

He had looked across the table at Shaw, at Aschenblum, at Popeye. Shaw was tight-lipped and stoic, Aschenblum looked puzzled, Popeye brooded, rotating an empty capsule between his fingers.

"Gentlemen, " Popeye had said, lifting his head, "what have we learned?"

A laugh burst out of Benjamin. "We've learned that we're a pack of *buffoons!*"

Popeye looked at Benjamin coolly. "We knew that already. Guys: we went through R&D, we examined the Pharma operation. We saw what we saw. What have we *learned?* From an operational perspective."

"From an *operational* perspective--!" sputtered Benjamin.

"Benjamin, please," said Popeye, suddenly the wise, patriarchal elder, the man who had seen it all. "We have to assess things calmly and see things as they are. There is never any other option."

Benjamin nodded. Popeye was right, of course, thought Benjamin. Especially right now. They had to assess their situation soberly. It was too dire for self-indulgent emotional outbursts.

Aschenblum spoke for Singh. "As far as the Chococoa R&D area goes, we learned nothing. They're not hiding anything; there's nothing *worth* hiding. They're mis-funded, unambitious. There's nothing wrong with the operation *per se*. It just doesn't appear to be contributing much of anything. They're merely going through the motions."

"And Pharma?"

Aschenblum leaned forward. "They seem to be doing nothing too. The materials I examined, the materials they've been shipping in, appear to be common materials used in pharmaceutical manufacture. Nothing particularly special. Certainly nothing to hide."

"Did you notice *anything* unusual?"

Aschenblum reflected. "Well—yes, actually. They have a tremendous amount of coffee beans."

"Coffee beans?"

"They drink a great deal of coffee?" said Benjamin. *"That's* the big secret?"

"They weren't drinking it, or even making coffee, really. They were processing the beans in order to extract caffeine. "

"Caffeine?"

"100% caffeine."

Shaw shrugged. "Why is that unusual? Some people don't like the taste of coffee. So there are pharmaceutical houses that make caffeine pills. Instead of drinking two or three cups of coffee, you swallow it in the form of a pill. What's the big deal?"

"But they were processing it—strangely," said Aschenblum.

"Why strangely?" said Popeye.

A puzzled expression crossed Aschenblum's face. "Caffeine extract has a typical color and granularity. Pharma seems to be aiming at a particular shade and texture."

"What for?"

"Who knows? It's just that—well, caffeine is like aspirin. Aspirin is aspirin. Powdered aspirin is powdered aspirin. Who makes exceptionally fine *pale pink* powdered aspirin? There isn't any market for *designer* versions of the stuff that I'm aware of. Or for 'designer caffeine.' At first I didn't even realize it *was* caffeine powder because it looked, well, off."

Popeye turned his head and pointed sharply at Benjamin. "Ben. You've been talking to that Christien girl?"

"We don't call women in business 'girls' anymore, Popeye," said Benjamin.

"At my age Cleopatra's mummy is a girl. That ain't what I'm asking."

"Yes. I have."

"She handles our distribution and theirs. Ask her where their stuff goes. To what companies."

"That may be proprietary information."

"Wine her. Dine her. Bribe her. I don't care. Find out."

At some point Benjamin had already decided to wine her and dine her, but that was the moment that Nicola walked in.

The expression she gave to attendees at board meetings was typically cool. Her expression now was arctic. She walked to the head of the table, placed her briefcase on it, opened it, pursed her lips, and then stared at the men at the other end of the table.

"I won't berate you gentlemen for the damage your senseless undertaking has cost this company," she began. "I doubt you intended it. From what the police tell me, the initial cause of the fires may even have been deliberate sabotage. In any case it is a loss Chococoa cannot sustain. I have sent an encrypted email to the address of the buyer offering to purchase Chococoa. I informed the buyer of the losses we've endured and are likely to continue to sustain as lawsuits from the Pharma organization are launched, as they surely will be. We must assume that the buyer's offer will be withdrawn. Therefore, Benjamin, I am provisionally instructing you to draw up papers for the firm's bankruptcy."

Benjamin opened his mouth to speak.

"But first," said Nicola, interrupting, looking them all in the eye, "I would like to know something. I am the chief executive officer of Chococoa Enterprises Limited. *I* make the final decisions. *I* authorize surprise incursions into internal operations—and I would *never* have authorized *any* such incursion into a *partnering* company's *independent* operations. Why did all of you go *behind my back?*"

No one was willing to be the first to answer.

Benjamin's phone rang.

"It's, uh, Johanna. From Ghana."

Nicola's icy gaze was unflinching.

"Patch her in. She deserves to see what a wreck you've all made."

Benjamin pressed an app and Johanna's voice rang through the air.

"Hello?" said Johanna.

"Johanna?"

"Hi, Benjamin."

"Hi," said Benjamin. "Johanna... "

"Yes, Benjamin?"

"Johanna... Jo, we did the inspections... "

"Yes, Benjamin."

"And... and it was a disaster. A *disaster*. There was an explosion. A fire. The Pharma section is—it's gone. All burned away. It spread to R&D. It's a total loss. We're certain to be sued. Johanna, I'm *so sorry...*"

She nodded.

"Jacob's been kidnapped," said Johanna. A moment passed, and then she said it again.

"Jacob's been kidnapped."

The connection broke.

"Johanna," cried Benjamin. "Johanna!"

The men exploded into questions as Benjamin frantically tried to call back and reach his sister.

Nicola stood there. Her face was expressionless, but an icy fury gathered in her eyes. She closed her suitcase, slowly and calmly, and looked around the boardroom for the very last time and walked to the door, put her hand on the knob, and opened it. She turned.

"Benjamin," she said.

But Benjamin's frantic attempts to reach Johanna on his phone went on. Everyone had questions, comments. Benjamin answered in panicked fits and starts.

"*What* happened?" said Shaw.

"Johanna was rammed earlier by a motorcycle," said Benjamin, "When they first arrived."

"You think there's a connection?" said Popeye.

"I don't know, I *don't know*."

Nicola calculated.

Johanna assaulted. Jacob kidnapped.

The Anans were being targeted.

"*Benjamin!*" she said sharply.

All the men's chatter and questions stopped at once.

"I'm resigning as chief executive of this company. Effective immediately."

2

Nicola stepped into the company vehicle.

"Take me to the airport," she said.

She had already made reservations along the way. There was no time for a commercial flight. A private plane was waiting. She would be in Ghana in a matter of hours.

So much for Plan A, she thought.

Plan A had been simple. Take Chococoa out of

Kwaku's corrupt hands by quietly putting it out of business. A neglect of inefficiencies here, a failure of maintenance there, a lack of preparedness in the event of inevitable market fluctuations. Chococoa would decay, close shop, and the pieces pass into other hands. But the Anans would be safe, and financially secure. And most importantly, they would not be objects of interest to Kwaku. Not corrupted or terrorized by Kwaku. As she had been. Very slight, very tiny and untraceable pointers on her part would draw attention to Freedom For The Children. That would implode too. She could not be certain the authorities would follow the trail to Kwaku, much less stop him, but they would hinder him. *Cost* him. Handled slowly enough, carefully enough, over a long enough time, no single element would point back to Nicola. She too might—*might*—escape the inevitable.

It was a good plan. It had been unfolding really well.

But now this.

How unfortunate.

She lifted her smartphone and put it to her ear.

Time for Plan B.

Kwaku's phone rang.

In Ghana, Kwaku was reading a biography of Napoleon over few Cognacs.

His phone murmured a soothing series of beeps. He looked at it.

Nicola.

Hm.

Ah well. Calls from Nicola could be amusing.

He lifted it and pressed the button.

"Yes?"

"I *told* you never to *touch* the Anan family!" she shouted.

"Dear me. Such a tone. That time of month again?"

"I told you to leave them alone!"

Kwaku sighed. "My dear. The Anan family exists— *you* exist—purely and solely because it is my pleasure.

213

You are all chess pieces whom I leave on the board because you may have some small part to play in future gambits. Do you actually not see that yet? Must I leave the head of one of your beloved Anans on your kitchen table some morning?"

"We have an *understanding*, you pompous ass."

"Yes," said Kwaku. "I command. You obey."

"I won't tolerate this," said Nicola.

"You will tolerate it," said Kwaku "because you have neither the power nor the courage to do anything else."

He could hear her breathing heavily and passionately, and chuckled. He delighted in Nicola's fury. That *cold* exterior. Kwaku could make her gibber like a chimp from the interior. It amused him no end.

"But, forgive me," said Kwaku. "How, specifically, have I *infringed* on the serenity of the Anans?"

"You had someone on a motorcycle ram Johanna Anan. You could have *killed* her."

"Oh that. Don't be silly. If I had *wanted* to kill her, she'd be dead! That was just a little tap. A reminder."

"Of *what?*"

"Of my *presence*. My capacities."

"And what about Jacob?"

Kwaku looked at the image of Napoleon on the cover of the book he was reading. The noble gaze. The strong world-historical stare. How he *transcended* the trivial humanity around him. For a moment Kwaku genuinely regretted what he done about Jacob. All of it was so very much beneath him.

"What do I care about petty little bugs like the Anans? Or, for that matter, cockroaches like yourself? I have deeper matters to consider."

Nicola could hear from the arrogance in his voice, even greater than normal, that he had been drinking. Good. Good.

"I want you to *leave them alone*," she shouted; no, she *commanded*.

He laughed. "Well! Come to my office and *debase*

yourself at long long last, *Darling*, and we'll see if I will! *Au revoir*."

He hung up.

Nicola switched off.

That went well. Quite well.

Kwaku liked feeling in control. He liked putting others at an emotional disadvantage, making them angry, upset, terrified. He felt comfortable that way.

She wanted him to feel comfortable and in charge and superior. To let his guard down.

In the evening distance she could see the private jet arriving, silhouetted against the sky.

3

Johanna lay on a cot in a cell in the Ghana Police Hospital on Ring Road East. The blue stars of the badges had gradually been replaced with red crosses and white nun-like headbands. Doctors had examined her, police had questioned her. When she mentioned the name Kwaku, they had looked at one another and said that they would come again. As the prepared to go, one of the younger officers leaned close to her ear and said, "Missy, you should go away from Ghana for a while."

A CAT scan showed no damage from her fall into the street. She asked for her phone and got it. Benjamin had been placing one call after another. They talked. Every sentence described one disaster after another.

We've failed, thought Johanna.

We've failed.

We've lost everything.

Even Jacob.

Tears ran down her cheeks, and were soon followed by aching sobs.

4

The taxi taking Nicola to the offices of Freedom For The Children stopped for a moment in an obscure alley. It was night, and a gentle rain fell, reflecting the lights and the neon of Accra with a gem-like subtlety. The contact she had been waiting for arrived. They spoke, and they made an exchange. She got back in the taxi and it resumed its path to Freedom For The Children. When the taxi finally arrived at its destination, she did not disembark immediately. She looked up at the tall skyscraper. She had lied to the taxi driver. Freedom For The Children was not her destination. He would never have driven her to her real destination. For above the charity's offices, taking up the entire higher floor, were Kwaku's Accra headquarters. Or, to be precise, his private residence, its luxury shared with one of his several command centers. If he were anywhere, it would be here.

She was not familiar with its inner sanctum. Perhaps no one was. The rumor was that Kwaku had killed the interior designers. The rumors were also that the walls were made of plate steel, that there were dissection rooms and torture chambers, chambers of child sex slaves. She knew the latter story was false. She and Kwaku had had several conversations over the years. He had suffered as a child, and *personally resented* those who made children suffer, a resentment that had left scores of child traffickers in Ghana dead. Their deaths had been... creative.

Since their first, horrible, meeting, Kwaku had invited her here several times. 'Invitation' was perhaps not the best term. 'Kidnapped and deposited' described an early such encounter.

Yet once deposited he had been relatively polite, questioning, even thoughtful. He was interested in in her public relations skills—her *artistry*, as he called it. He too was an artist, he announced, and his masterpiece was *Kwaku*, a brooding demonic figure permeating all Ghana like a miasma. Nicola had lent her art to his: better to seem a moral monstrosity than be one.

But of course Kwaku was both. That was the problem.

Pinpricks of rain burst on the windows of the taxi. The evening neons of Accra danced and refracted through them. How lovely, she thought. She realized in a few moments more she would probably be dead. The rain, the cool night air, the lights of Accra—seeing them all, seeing *the world*, for perhaps the last time, touched and moved her. Most of all the skyscraper moved her— the skyscraper, the embodiment of achievement and ambition, of human reason.

She thought, strangely enough, of Johanna—Johanna, the builder. She would miss their arguments.

She placed a call to Kwaku.

She was here.

To debase herself.

His chuckle was rich. He told her to step outside in the rain. She took up her briefcase, paid the driver, and did so.

In a moment the hulking bodyguard appeared, and took her through the doors into the building. How long had she known him, this bald terrifying rhinoceros of a figure? In all that time he had never spoken a single word. Spot checks, metal detectors, all of that was waved aside. She was visiting Kwaku, and Kwaku's visitors were not bound by the rules. Security guards looked the other way as they passed. Only a fool would keep Kwaku waiting just to check an ID.

They entered Kwaku's private elevator and rose to his private floor.

They exited. Nicola and the bodyguard moved automatically in the direction of what passed for a conference room, the room where she had first met Kwaku. Along the way a sudden blood-curdling scream rang out from behind a door. Torture? A recording? Kwaku so loved playing on people's *nerves*. Nicola's face was expressionless.

They came to a door. The bodyguard opened it. Nicola stepped inside.

At the far end of the boardroom table sat Kwaku in a brilliant white shirt and a red paisley evening robe, nursing a goblet of champagne.

The light, for once, played fully on Kwaku's horrific features. Nicola, the mistress of appearances, generally tried to look beyond appearances. It was impossible in this case. Those features were as sickening as the person beneath them. In his elegant robe he looked like some radioactive mutation introducing the next episode of Masterpiece Theatre.

"Nicola, how wonderful of you to stop by," he purred. "Would you like to be debased now, or after some Zinfandel?"

Nicola put her briefcase on the conference table and snapped the locks.

"Business first," she said, "Chococoa Ltd is going into bankruptcy," she began, "and as a result— "

She took out a custom-designed traceable pistol and put five bullets into Kwaku's chest.

She pivoted instantly and put a bullet into the guard, whose own Glock was already out.

It had been very close, but Nicola's bullet struck first, hitting the guard in the shoulder and slamming him to the ground.

Nicola took another clip out of her briefcase, slapped it into her gun, and walked over and pointed the gun at the bodyguard's face.

But for a moment, for the very first time, the face was human, and in pain, and the eyes pleaded; said, *please, no.*

She reached down, took his gun, and put it into her briefcase. Then she turned, and looked at the twisted features at Kwaku, sitting gnarled upon his throne like some obscene swastika. His shirt was a white expanse blossoming with the roses of his blood.

She turned and left, going down the private elevator,

quickly and silently walking out of the building into the gleaming Accra night.

5

A police officer accompanied by a nurse entered the room. Johanna looked up from her bed.

The officer was an unsmiling hard-faced man with a scar along his left cheek. He had seen a good deal of things that men should not see, and it had left his face a grim grizzled mask. Johanna's heart sank. One look was enough to tell her what she feared. She felt the tears already coming to her eyes, but held them back.

The nurse tried to introduce the officer gently, but he cut in, brusque and to the point.

"You know this boy?" he said.

He held out his smartphone.

There was a photograph on it.

It was the face of Jacob. His features appeared smudged with smoke and ash. His head seemed to be resting on a floor. His cheeks were hollow.

His eyes were closed.

Jacob!

Johanna's control dissolved. It was like a dam shattering. She broke into tears.

"Do you *know* this boy?" said the officer, irritated.

Johanna nodded. She could not speak.

"Can you identify him?"

She nodded.

"Jacob Anan. Is that correct?"

Her heart withered within her.

"Y-yes," she whispered.

"Well, *thank* you," barked the officer. "Damned women," he mumbled. "Can't ever give you a straight yes and no."

He made a note on a keyboard phone app.

"You can visit him in Recovery in about an hour,"

said the officer. "The nurse can take you down."

"*He's alive?*"

The officer raised an eyebrow. "He was never reported dead. Just missing." He put away his phone. "He's alive. He's under observation. Smoke inhalation. Rope burns. Probably be in bed here for several days."

Johanna lurched out of bed. The nurse stopped her.

"He's fine, dear. He's fine!"

6

Johanna opened the door and stepped into the boardroom. On the plane she had fallen in and out sleep fitfully time and again. Every dream was a nightmare, and now this, reality, was one nightmare more. As in a dream, the faces of people long known surrounded her, the settings were the same, but distorted and surreal, reality and yet not.

Was it really a month ago that she had been given the assignment to analyze the company's operations and by so doing save it? No, only several days had passed; several days for everything, the company, her father's legacy, to collapse into irretrievable ruin.

She had no regrets. Jacob was alive. The tight-lipped officer had grudgingly explained that there had been a tractor-trailer fire. Based on the way the lock has professionally been broken into, the police believed local gang members may have been trying to break into it. They found a fire just starting, clouds of smoke, and Jacob tied to a chair. Surprisingly, at least to the officer, they pulled him out. Perhaps they thought he was an outsider like them, not someone worth kidnapping. Who knows? They pulled him out and then just vanished. The police got an anonymous call, and drove out, and there he was.

Kwaku, thought Johanna. *Kwaku said he would give Jacob back to her. He must have sent someone.*

When she saw Jacob in Recovery she threw herself over him like a blanket. He half-coughed after every other word.

But he was alive. *Alive!*

But that ecstasy of a few days ago, the joy of the whole family, had soon been replaced by another feeling. The realization that while Jacob was alive, Chococoa was dead.

Chococoa was dead, and she had failed.

Complete, total, utter failure.

Failure.

She took her seat, fighting back tears, and looked around at the faces around her.

"Hi Jo," said Benjamin quietly.

Across from him Popeye nodded. Graham, Chief of Operations was not there. Shaw, the Chief of Security, was supposed to be attending, but wasn't. *Maybe they've quit,* thought Johanna bitterly. *Rats desert a sinking ship.*

At least Noelle Christien was there, sitting next to Benjamin and looked up at Johanna with deep sympathy. It made sense for her to be here, Johanna supposed. The dissolution of their business would affect hers.

Jacob was not in attendance. He was still being examined by medical people in Ghana and still being interviewed by police making out reports. But he was recovering, and would be back soon. Thank God. A silver lining in the cloud. The family business was done, but at least the family survived.

But for how long? The bills for her father's care had suddenly spiked astronomically a year ago. The spike had passed, but did that suggest that more strokes were on the way? With the business gone, could they continue that level of care if Pharma sued them individually?

Their financial picture was about to change radically. She took a deep breath. She needed to focus. To think and act like a professional.

"Where's Chris?" she said. "We need to see the numbers."

Popeye spoke up. "Chris is in police custody."

"*What?*"

"The police arrested him yesterday."

"*Chris?*" she said. "Where's Nicola?" said Johanna.

Benjamin and Popeye looked at each other.

"She tendered her resignation the day before yesterday," said Benjamin. "We haven't been able to reach her since."

She looked from one to the other.

"Then—who's running the company?"

Benjamin attempted to answer, and the words failed to come out. Noelle put her hand on his.

He cleared his throat.

"Technically," he said, "no one."

His iPhone rang.

"Hi, Naomi. Yes. Yes, she's here." Benjamin nodded. "Yes, we're ready."

Benjamin looked around at the people at the table and said, "Naomi is bringing in the buyer. She says he's still interested in buying the company—though at a greatly reduced price. She feels we have no choice but to accept. Also…" he slipped a look at Johanna. "Naomi thinks that Father should be here. She's bringing him in in the wheelchair."

Johanna bowed her head. Yes, that was proper. That was appropriate, He was there at the beginning of the company. It was proper that he should be there at the end. She was only sorry that, at some level, he would witness her shame and her failure.

Her teeth ground. There, on her laptop in her briefcase, was a simulation model of the operations of Chococoa Ltd. All the processes had been gone over, all the linkages duly described, masses of notes had been added on small ways to optimize this and accelerate that. Her observations, and the comments of the managers she had talked to and the workers she had worked alongside, and even the comments of the end users on social media and in focus groups that Nicola had relentlessly compiled and translated into statistics. She hadn't had time to compile it into a report or a presentation, but it was all *there*: the portrait a fully functioning, fully sustainable, profit-generating company. Even with all the challenges it faced and was facing, Chococoa was still viable. Or had been, a few days ago, when she was here the last time.

And now? The CEO vanished, the Finance Officer arrested, part of the company a burnt-out ruin, a Partner suing them, the owner selling.

She covered her face in her hands.

Had she been wrong? Should she have taken Kwaku's offer?

The door opened.

Naomi wheeled Michael Anan into the room in his wheelchair. He had a plaid Scottish blanket over his legs and Naomi had seen that he was dressed quite elegantly in a business suit and tie, and a tasteful scarf. His eyes were closed, and his head was bent. He seemed as though he were asleep, and almost smiling at a pleasant dream. Johanna's heart simply burst with love for him.

Popeye stood up and went to the head of the table and pulled the Director's chair one spot to the side. Naomi smiled at him in appreciation. Yes, Michael should sit at the very head. She placed him there, and smoothed his hair.

She looked at them all with a strange, joyous expression.

"This executive meeting of Chococoa Enterprises, Ltd., is now called to order," she said. "As you all know, under the terms of founding of this company, in the event that the founding owner, Michael Anan, is incapacitated, ownership is passed along to his wife, which is to say, to me. Some weeks ago Chococoa received an offer to buy the firm. In my capacity as owner, and before legal witnesses, I now wish to accept that offer and sell the company."

Benjamin broke the silence.

"May I ask what the buyer has agreed to pay?"

Michael Anan lifted his head and opened his eyes.

"One Euro," he said.

He looked around with a big grin.

Then, to the complete and utter astonishment of everyone seated, he placed both his hands on the arms of his armchair, shifted, pushed himself up a little shakily, and rose to his feet.

He took a Euro out of his pocket and gave it to a smiling, crying Naomi.

"Here you go," he said. "I expect a receipt, now!"

He looked around. "Well? Cat got your tongues?"

Johanna and Benjamin tore out of their seats at once and threw themselves around their father. Tears streamed from their eyes, incoherent cries from their lips. They laughed, cried, babbled, embraced.

"*How*—?

"*What*—?"

"*Papa!*"

Anan laughed. "Careful, careful! You'll knock over mywheelchair!"

He gave his son and daughter a last big hug, and said, "Help me sit down," and Benjamin instantly complied, settling his father back into the wheelchair.

"How in the *world*—?" said Benjamin.

Michael Anan patted him on the arm, and Johanna as well, and said, "I'll explain everything. Sit down, sit down!"

The two didn't return to their previous seats. They couldn't tear themselves away. Everyone at the table pulled their chairs over and gathered around Michael.

He looked at them all and laughed and clapped his hands. Joy radiated from him.

"All of you, it's so *good* to talk to you all again."

"*How?*" said Benjamin.

"Well," said Michael Anan. "it was Nicola, really. About a year ago the doctors tried a new experimental drug—a variant on something called 'Edonerpic

Maleate.' They though it would help."

"And it *cured* you?" said Johanna.

"They administered it to me for several months. It appeared to have no effect whatsoever."

"Then how—?"

"Nicola visited me regularly. Naomi told her about the drug, and its apparent lack of effect, and Nicola told Naomi about an episode of *House M.D.* that she had once seen. Everyone assumed that a cure that should have worked had simply failed. But the truth was that the cure *had* worked. The symptoms were still being maintained by a completely different illness that no one had tested for. She told Naomi to have me tested for diseases other than stroke than could mimic paralysis. Specifically ones common to Ghana and Ghanaians. I'd grown up there, you know. Naomi took Nicola's suggestion to heart, God bless her," said Michael, reaching out and taking Naomi's hand, and patting it.

"It turned out that the new medication *had* resolved the stroke. I'd been recovering across the board.! However ther was an additional autoimmune disease I can't pronounece that I'd contracted. *That* was producing the paralysis that everyone *assumed* was the result of stroke. Once the autoimmune disease was treated, the paralysis vanished, and the effects of new medication started becoming apparent almost at once."

"You can't imagine how I felt," said Naomi, holding Michael's hand against her cheek. "One day he just *opened his eyes*. He said—'Naomi.'"

"Why didn't you *tell* us?" said Benjamin.

"Don't blame her, Benjamin. I didn't want you to know. I wasn't able to talk like this for months. I didn't want you to see me struggling for words, not able to pick up a pencil, or get to my feet. Besides, the drug was experimental. I didn't know if it would wear off, and if I'd slip back. I asked Naomi to tell no one, absolutely no one, till I could get back to my feet.

"And," said Michael Anan. "I wanted to see

something."

"What?"

"I wanted to see how you all handled the business in my absence."

Johanna turned her face away.

"I'm so sorry, Papa," she whispered bitterly. "I failed. I failed at everything."

Michael put his hand on Johanna's head. "What are you talking about, you silly girl? You've done *wonderfully*. All of you. I couldn't be more proud!"

"Proud? But the company—everything's a complete *disaster*."

He laughed.

"How so?"

"The company was put up for *sale!*"

"Yes, I just bought it. Naomi, show her the Euro."

"The *fire!*"

"There's a thing we occasionally make use of in business these days, Johanna. Haven't you heard of it? It's called 'insurance'."

"We're underwater financially, Papa," said Benjamin. "Very much so."

"The *business*, yes," said Michael Anan. "But not the owner. And when you're confined to a wheelchair, Benjamin, people read to you a good deal. When you're recovering, you do a good deal of reading yourself. I read the *Financial Post* religiously, as well as a number of books on the futures market. Even before the stroke, I could see that the market was going into stormy weather, and was likely to go way down. So I sold short."

"So the worst things got for Chococoa—"

"—the better things got for my portfolio. That's exactly right. And my portfolio is a *very* impressive one at this point. I could fund the recovery of this company personally if need be. But there's no need. The banks treated me well before. If they know Michael Anan is back in the CEO spot, I'm sure we can re-negotiate or arrange loans on much better terms. I've already sent out a few feelers. I'd rather do it that way than spend my funds directly—after a big fall, there's always a rise, and my current investments are all set to go for a ride in the upper direction now. Good for me, good for Chococoa."

"But we're still facing serious law suits, Papa," said Benjamin.

"Oh?" said Anan. "Naomi, give me your iPhone."

He pressed a button. "Mr. Shaw? Could you come in now, please?"

Chief of Security Shaw walked in. A smile spread over his face. "You've let them in on the big secret, I see. Now *that's* what a happy family looks like."

He and Anan shook hands. "Welcome back, Boss!" said Shaw.

"Thank you," said Michael. "And thank you for waiting till we had our little reunion.

"I didn't want to get trampled as they ran over to you!"

"What's the latest news?" said Michael.

"Pretty much what we expected. Many thanks to you, Benjamin. You especially, Popeye."

"Benjamin has a private investigator that he uses," explained Michael to Johanna.

"I had him look into Nicola and her finances," said Benjamin. "I know, I know, it was uncalled for, but the situation—"

"It *was* uncalled for," said Michael, "Nicola's finances, and her handling of company finances, have always been immaculate."

"But the investigator did find something odd," said Benjamin. "Instead of keeping her personal funds in the bank, she seemed to be putting a lot of it, in fact nearly *all* of it, into Bitcoin."

"Cryptocurrencies?" said Johanna. "That's unusual, but there's nothing criminal about it."

"No," said Benjamin. "But Johanna's background is Marketing and Psychology. Where did she learn enough to invest in crytpocurrencies at a high level?

The investigator decided to look further, and decided that she probably had picked the brain of our resident geek, Chris. He looked into Chris's background, and found a *long* trail of cryptocurrency use, including many involving Silk Road."

"I remember that name," said Johanna. "Wasn't that some kind of online drug exchange?"

Shaw nodded. "And how. You could buy all the drugs in the world at Silk Road, and the only currency they accepted was Bitcoin. The investigator poked around various online forums, and learned that Chris had a number of different usernames that he chatted under. One of those names made a lot of Silk Road purchases for Adderall and other 'smart' drugs while it was in operation. Drugs supposed to increase IQ, alertness, intellectual performance."

"That certainly fit Chris," said Naomi. Heads nodded. Chris had been nothing if not brilliant, hyper, and just a little strange.

"He discussed smart drugs with a few other people in the forums. This was a few years ago, when Chris was barely out of college, and the people he talked to were still students. The investigator checked the online usernames and began matching them to usage elsewhere and then to actual people. One of the people went on to form a startup manufacturing smart drugs."

"Ah," said Noelle suddenly. "Of course!"

They looked at her. "A startup called Big Pharma. Yes?"

"Yes," said Shaw.

"That's when it all clicked," said Popeye. "Noelle, you did the distribution for Big Pharma, you were aware of what they were shipping, right?"

"Of course," she said. "Drugs are not shipped over several borders blindly. The materials sent were principally materials used in the manufacture of prescription drugs for other companies."

"With the exception of—?"

"The caffeine," said Noelle. "We would receive and deliver large amounts of coffee beans to the Chococoa facility. But when the time came to distribute their output, neither coffee nor caffeine was part of it. The caffeine would go in, but never out. It was curious."

"Yeah. Curious," said Popeye. He fished a hand into his shirt pocket and took out a capsule with finely ground contents the color of a pale rose. "Recognize this?" he said, tossing it to Noelle.

"It is their premiere product," said Noelle. "A prescription drug intended to enhance cognitive function and alertness called Cognizac Omega Z."

"You got to love the guy they hire to name things at that place," said Popeye. "How much for one pill?"

"Nearly £850. Nearly $1000 US dollars," said Noelle.

"You're joking," said Benjamin. "Who would pay that?"

"Any extremely wealthy family that thinks that a pill like Cognizec before the exam will get their brat into Oxford or Cambridge or Johns Hopkins. Pop *this* baby and you will get *alert*. Fast," said Popeye.

He reached into his shirt pocket and pulled out another capsule with pale rose contents.

"And you know what? Pop *this* pill and you will get alert fast too. Real fast," said Popeye.

Johanna took the pill and looked at it. "It looks like the other pill," she said.

"Yeah," said Popeye. "Except the first pill is Cognizac Omega Z, and the pill Johanna is holding is caffeine. It's *pretty* caffeine. Look, it's all pink! Down in the Pharma installation they would add dye and make it pretty and pink, and put it in a capsule just like this other pill. Not like boring old regular, white, caffeine powder."

Noelle clapped her hands together, and rolled her eyes.

"You got it, Mademoiselle," said Popeye. "They make this knockoff version for less than penny, slip it into a prescription bottle with the regular stuff, and boom: instant £850 more profit per bottle! How's the user supposed to know the difference? They still get the same jolt. Hell, it's like drinking six cups of coffee! Pop three and you'll fly to the moon! Or who knows, maybe they just sell the pills on the black market *as* Cognizac. What street buyer is going to do a chemical analysis?"

"Drug Enforcement is looking for heroin and cocaine and all the typical street drugs. They don't catch it because when it comes in with all the other material from Ghana, it's just caffeine."

"And when it goes out," said Noelle, "It's *still* just caffeine. A little color has been added, but what of it?"

"Except somewhere further along the supply chain they slap a little 'Z' on the capsule and the price jumps nearly a thousand dollars." Popeye laughed. "You know, there must have been thousands of those pills down there. Once on the market, that's what—five, ten million dollars?" He whistled. "Nice."

Shaw nodded. "At some point after Chris' old friend on the smart drug forums started Big Pharma, he must have proposed the arrangement to Chris. And then Chris proposed renting the space and some equipment to Nicola. It was reasonable; it made economic sense."

"Nicola didn't know," said Benjamin. "According to my investigator, she didn't receive so much as one farthing off the books."

"Neither did Chris, I hear," said Shaw.

"What?" said Johanna.

"I have a contact. Chris confessed. He claims he didn't know what they were doing in the Pharma section. He says Pharma just wanted a place to colorize the caffeine off-site, and his friend said that if he could arrange the deal, they'd give him a free supply of Cognizac for as long as they were there."

"So they paid him in smart drugs."

"They paid him in *pink caffeine!*" laughed Shaw. "What the hell. If one pill equaled six cups of Dark Roast and he downed three at a time, who could tell the difference?"

"But he didn't know that."

"No," said Shaw. "He did not. He thought he had hundreds of illegal prescription drugs in his stash in his locker in the Pharma section. And he was probably hyper on his pills already. When he heard we were doing an inspection, he panicked. He went to his car. He had a can of oil and a can of gas, and matches in the glove compartment. He poured one into the other, capped it, put it in his suitcase and walked back in, suited up, put it in his stash locker and lit the match. Two minutes later, and—boom. Goodbye evidence."

"He should have just grabbed the pills and left."

"With us and Security standing there with our smartphones?" said Shaw. "When you're doing a surprise inspection, you don't let people grab bags of stuff and run out the door with it."

"So much chaos over so little," said Noelle. "How sad. Poor little man."

"Lucky little man," said Shaw. "The police say the caffeine levels in his blood were so high he's suffering from the kind of chronic hypertension that produces massive heart attacks. His panic attack got him arrested, but the arrest probably saved his life."

"And killed our company."

"Oh, not at all," said Michael Anan. "Am I right, Mr. Shaw?"

Shaw smiled. "Right you are, Mr. Anan. Once Popeye added one and one together—the pink caffeine and the items Ben's investigator uncovered—we called Interpol. Big Pharma has a new name again: Dead Meat. They've been shut down. They won't be suing anyone."

Benjamin straightened. He looked around, as though he'd realized something. He had.

"This means—"

Johanna completed his sentence. "This means the company is saved," she said simply.

"Why, yes," said Michael. "Didn't I say that already?" He looked over at Naomi. "Children," he said. "They never listen."

"I guess this means a bonus for Popeye," said Popeye.

"I guess this means a celebration," said Benjamin, slipping his arm into the arm of Noelle.

"No," said Johanna, slapping her hand on the table. "This means we can start getting this company to operate *right!*" She pulled open her computer. "I've been going over *every inch* of our Ghana operations, and plugging in data about *every step* of our supply chain, and taking *thousands* of notes, Papa, and there are *hundreds* of improvements—"

"*Johanna!*" said Michael sharply.

"—What, Papa?"

"You're hired," he said. "Starting tomorrow. *Tonight* I have special reservations for dinner for all of us, and the cuisine is specially prepared. Benjamin, call the cars around. It's Ghana Night in Derby!"

7

After a minute or two had passed, the eyes of Kwaku's bodyguard fluttered, and his massive body half-rolled over. With a grimace of pain, the massive figure got to one knee, and at length finally stood.

Kwaku...

He was a believer. He was one of those who regarded Kwaku as not a man at all, but a demon, a demon playing at being a man. He had seen inexplicable things. But now all he saw was a bloody torso underneath a mass of unmoving scar tissue.

Had Kwaku been only a man all along?

Kwaku's head jerked straight up.

He began laughing maniacally, like The Riddler.

The bodyguard froze in terror.

Kwaku clapped his hands and laughed till he began to choke. "*Nicola!* Nicola, bravo!" He laughed. "You *did* debase yourself. Wonderful! Oh this has been a *thrilling* evening! And to think of how tediously it started off."

The bodyguard shook with horror. *The demon could not die!* The huge man lost control; a stain on his pants appeared as he wet himself. He fell to his knees and bowed before the demon Kwaku.

"Oh, get up and go find a doctor. You've been shot, you idiot. *Go!*" said Kwaku.

The bodyguard fled, terrified. Ghana would ring later tonight with more murmured stories of Kwaku, Kwaku the Demon who, riddled with bullets, rose from the dead and *laughed.*

Meanwhile, alone in the conference room, Kwaku took off his robe, and his shirt, and the bulletproof vest underneath it. Inspired by Nicola, he always wore the vest covered with plastic bags of bright red animal blood. He had used it to stage his death and resurrection before, and maintained the practice. The effect on the criminal public and his underlings had been simply marvelous. Normally he didn't bother with it, particularly not when dealing with a prima donna like Nicola, but she had arrived unexpectedly, and while he might wave such a private guest in casually, he was not a complete fool.

He still laughed as he prepared himself another Zinfandel. No, he thought—a Napoleon brandy! This was an evening to celebrate. That *pristine little rationalist* had gambled wildly. The *boring ethicist* had sunk to murder! Well, all right, attempted murder, but what of it? Kwaku had *corrupted* her—and was that not the signature of a devil? After all this time he had finally *won.* He felt positively giddy.

And what now? Would he track her down and have her killed? He supposed he ought to. One had professional traditions to maintain. But there was no hurry. Freedom For The Children had largely run its course. Questions from Interpol, from tax investigators, from journalists had begun to accumulate. It had had its day. And Chococoa appeared to be on its last legs too. Why take over a dying business when you could take over a living rising one? He was already looking beyond these things. The snake must shed his skin and find another.

But—Nicola? He smiled. What a *brave*, reckless creature! She had actually given her master, Kwaku, a *surprise!* A *thrill!* He looked around the conference room and sipped his brandy and felt life coursing through him, and it felt *good* to be alive.

He lifted his glass to Nicola.

Yes, let the little lamb gambol free for a while. The lion would pounce in due course.

8

"A toast," said Michael Anan. "To Nicola."

They all stood. Johanna, Benjamin, Popeye, Shaw, the Cult. Even Jacob, astonished and delighted to see his father standing and talking, had been patched in onscreen via iPad.

Michael Anan stood at the head of a table overflowing with *Jollof* rice and *Banku* and *Waakye* and *Red-Red* and *Fufu* and *Tuo Zaafi* and *Kenkey* and *Kelewele* and *Omo Tuo* and *Kontomire* Stew and a dozen other delicacies that Noelle and Shaw and Popeye could not pronounce but that had stuffed them all like prize turkeys. Presiding over it all was the founder and newly restored President of Chococoa, and at a pause in the shouting and the laughter and the conversation, he rose. He seemed to take a particular pleasure in rising. He lifted his glass of champagne.

"To Nicola," said Michael, "wherever she may be."

Everyone drank. Except Johanna.

I was so wrong, she thought. All those arguments and disagreements. Yet they were here tonight—her father was standing there, laughing and smiling—only because of Nicola.

She thought too. Of Kwaku.

"I am not yet done with Nicola," he had said in that rich, awful, inhuman voice of his.

He was closing his interests in Chococoa, Ltd., he said. Did that mean that he considered that Nicola had failed him? If that was the case, she was under the earth now, bones broken and limbs dismembered. Johanna looked with pain into her champagne.

No, she would tell no one about that, or about Kwaku. Not one penny would be going to Freedom For The Children now. If it even existed any longer. She wouldn't tarnish Nicola's memory. She owed her far, far too much.

She lifted her glass of champagne, and drank it to the lees.

Thank you, Nicola, she thought. And wondered.

Epilogue

Arne Gnaarsaksen piloted his boat in the direction of the islet without a name. The district really needed to give the islet a name one of these days, he thought. True, Iceland had an incredible number of these little island-like stretches of land bobbing their heads up from the waters. But this one was actually owned by someone. A person actually lived there. Every three months he would fire up the motor of his tug and deliver foodstuffs and other items. If a person lived somewhere they ought to at least have an address. That's how Arne Gnaarsaksen saw things.

He shrugged, and lit his pipe. His startling blue eyes, wrinkling like cobwebs from a lifetime of staring into the wind and out at the sea, looked out again at the waves, at the Icelandic expanses of snow and shore. He had been told as a boy that the beauty would fade, that he would grow used to it with age. But the beauty only seemed to grow. When he looked out at it, a kind of great peace entered into his heart, like a foretaste of Eternity. He could sail along these white shores forever.

Eventually up ahead he saw the outline of the nameless islet; there, slowly, was the long and ramshackle-looking but sturdy pier. He pulled his ancient tug beside it, moored it with a rope, and began hauling his deliveries onto the planks. One box, a second, a third. Cans of food, fresh vegetables, books. Simple things. He checked the post box nailed to the side of the pier. There was the order for the next delivery. An international money order would be waiting when he got back home.

He looked up and, yes, there he was, high up in the distance, watching from behind a hill. He knew nothing about the owner, whom he thought of as The American. He thought of him as The American because he obviously had to be crazy to live out here alone like this. And who is crazier than Americans? Years ago there had been a Cold War tracking station on the islet. From the station the Americans could track the nuclear missiles from the USSR that they expected fly over any day and destroy the world. Bad luck, the world survived. The tracking station was stripped of its more sensitive equipment and abandoned.

And then a year or two ago some business entity purchased it, and Arne Gnaarsaksen and his family and a few local tradesmen had sailed in to sweep things up, put in drapes and furnishings, a refrigerator and transmitter, an artificial fireplace and signal boosters and a few carpets, and made it a home. A strange sort of home, but livable. And then one day the new resident was just there, looking down from the peak of the snowy dunes as Arne Gnaarsaksen made his deliveries.

The American was in a warm bulky suit and thick boots that guarded against the cold. The suit's hood was always up, the face always covered with a scarf, the eyes hidden behind goggles. On one occasion Arne Gnaarsaksen could see something in The American's hands. A rifle? That worried him. There was nothing to hunt around here but Arne Gnaarsaksen! But maybe it was a walking staff. The snow could be hard to walk through.

Arne Gnaarsaksen waved. He always waved. The

American always waved back. Once Arne Gnaarsaksen had tried to wave the figure over. Come down! Say hello! But The American had fanned his hands the way people do. *No, no.* Arne had shrugged. Well, some people just wanted to be alone, he supposed. Or perhaps the poor man was horribly disfigured. His family talked about him sometimes. Young Bjorn thought he was an alien from space. Arne Gnaarsaksen shook his head. Young people.

Arne Gnaarsaksen waved again. Goodbye. Goodbye, strange American. Goodbye, waved the strange American.

Arne Gnaarsaksen returned to his ship, re-started the motor, and turned around to go back home.

The American let twenty minutes pass, till Arne was not even a dot on the horizon, and then walked down to the pier.

When the figure arrived, he picked up the boxes—they were not too heavy—and reached around and took off a backpack. Inside was a rolled-up set of slats attached to a rope. The figure put the boxes on the slats, fastened them, and then dragged them off the pier and up the hill. There a sled sat waiting, and the figure put the boxes on the sled, pulled it about a mile to the tracking station, and got the boxes indoors.

Once the doors were closed, the figure pushed back the hood, removed the scarf, took off the goggles, unzipped the suit, and stepped out into the warm interior air.

Nicola Cavalcanti then went over to the sofa and pulled on a cardigan. She shook her hair freely. The coffee had been brewing long enough, and she could smell it. She went to the kitchen area and made herself a cup.

First things first. She checked the boxes for markings and found the ones with perishables. Vegetables were important! She put those away in the refrigerator immediately. Then she scrounged for toothpaste and Maxi pads and whatnot—but saw the books, and forgot everything else. Books, books! *Plays,* by George Bernard

Shaw. *Seven Science Fiction Novels*, by H. G. Wells. *What Ho, Jeeves!* By P. G. Wodehouse. *Reap*, a medical thriller. All of Haruki Murakami. An obscure book of poetry called *The Age of Steel*. The *Foundation* trilogy by Isaac Asimov. *The Count of Monte Cristo*. A Raymond Chandler. *The Power of Awareness* by Neville Goddard. *The Collected Poetry of Wallace Stevens*.

She broke into a smile of pure delight. That was enough unpacking for today! She went to her lumpy, comfortable sofa and plopped down and read till the sun began to sink and her eyes grew tired and she fell asleep.

Nicola woke up hours later, as waves of mystical light fanned magically around her. They seemed to run through every color of the rainbow, and some that rainbows had never heard of. Her eyelids fluttered, and uncurling on the sofa she turned and looked out the window. The Northern Lights!

She stood up and gazed out at the display. Astonishing! The waves of light played across the sky like brushstrokes painted by God. She could stare at them for hours, and sometimes did,

But regrettably they interfered with radio waves. Pity. She would miss her regular short-wave chess game with the old Viennese professor, and the forum discussion on LinkedIn on *Marketing and McLuhan*. But then she was nearly finished with her second book. A few distractions less meant a word count that came to more.

Nicola had spent a long time thinking about the meaning of peace of mind. The solitude here, the quiet; the sea, the skies, the white dunes of snow, all inclined a person to reflect. Peace of mind meant being free and independent. It meant freedom from stress, freedom from pressure, freedom from schedules and deadlines and targets, freedom from people. Benjamin had once called her a monk, and he had been right. Her beauty constantly drew attention to her, and she didn't want attention. She wanted learning and understanding. She wanted to be an independent scholar. To have the time to read, write, think. To live unmolested, unthreatened, without being *stared* at and bothered and chased.

She had gambled, that last time with Kwaku. She knew it was a gamble, that the gamble would likely fail, that if she survived at all she would either be hunted down by Kwaku or by the police. But if by some miracle she did survive, she wanted to place herself as far beyond her old life as she possibly could. To strip away all the extraneous things and live a life of pure and perfect peace and quiet and study. It took a great deal of time and careful effort to arrange.

Chris had shown her how to move her funds around without leaving any tracks whatsoever. She formed an entity in one nation within an entity in another nation inside a trust inside a Bitcoin-friendly third nation, and in the end she acquired an island all her own, with living facilities providing everything she might need, and an internet connection so deeply barricaded behind VPNs and Tor shells and private pirate servers that she could access the world, and yet could not be found.

On her islet there were no friendly faces, not physically, but online she had already made many new friends. And could follow old ones. Michael and Naomi were on their third honeymoon now. President Johanna Anan was indeed making Chococoa great again. Making it great while putting her foot in her mouth, as she did so often, but then that was Johanna, nothing if not blunt. Benjamin and Noelle had tied the knot, and a child was on the way! And Jacob was on the road to becoming a professor. Of Scottish literature, of all things. Where had *that* come from?

But they were thriving. That was all that counted.

And Kwaku. Somehow he had lived. How could he possibly have lived? But he had. She knew she should have shot him in the face. But that *face*. It was impossible to look directly into it. Impossible not to feel pity. And a moment's hesitation would have been fatal.

Prior to her last visit, she had written a long document detailing everything she knew, suspected, and intuited about Kwaku and his dealings and sent it in sealed envelopes to Interpol, to Police Headquarters in Ghana, to a variety of police and intelligence agencies around the world. She believed it would hurt him, and hurt him deeply. Perhaps it had. There was as little trace of him to be found as there was of her. Or perhaps he had grown so strong that nothing could touch him, no one dared mention him. Or perhaps he too had withdrawn, to re-assess, to think, to plan.

All that was part of her previous life, however. The life gone by. Her life was here now, the life of the mind, living in peace, surrounded by a world of amazing natural beauty. Perhaps she would tire of it one day, and return. And perhaps not.

All that she knew, looking at the shimmering lights dancing across the sky, was that she was happy.

The End

ABOUT THE AUTHOR

James Amoah was born in Accra, Ghana, with its mosaic of town life, rich Ghanaian culture, and personal history within which he was nurtured and inspired. He moved as a young child with his family to London, England. Studying his B.Sc. Pharmacology at Liverpool University, he then went on to gain his Masters in Operational Research at Lancaster University. He has spent the last decade of his life in Lausanne, Switzerland.

James is the CEO & Founder of *Kaleidoscope International Sarl*, a supply chain consultancy with over twenty years' experience of designing, managing and delivering complex supply chain and business turnaround programs. He has a deep passion for seeing the delivery of success and building strong teams. James has held several global senior positions in large multinationals, including International Vice President of Operations Management CareFusion and Executive Director Europe, Africa and Middle East (EAME) for Johnson & Johnson. He serves as a Board adviser to small and medium enterprises (SMEs) within healthcare, primarily in Switzerland, the UK and North America.

Kaleidoscope International Sarl is a niche Supply Chain Consultancy founded in 2013 and based in Lausanne, Switzerland. The company is focused on significantly improving its customers profitability and successful business operational changes. Kaleidoscope International, via its *Supply Chain Mastery Academy*, also offers uniquely successful approaches to differentiated supply chain learning and development training.

Find out more at www.kaleidoscope-int.com and/or at jamesamoah.com Or contact the author directly at supplychainnovel@gmail com.

Printed in Great Britain
by Amazon

53953430R00154